CALLED!

a LONGSHOT'S STORY

written by the

REV. DR. GORDON POSTILL

 FriesenPress

Suite 300 - 990 Fort St
Victoria, BC, V8V 3K2
Canada

www.friesenpress.com

Permission received from HarperCollins Publishers and Frederick Buechner Literary Assets, LLC to use one quote from Frederick Buechner's book *Telling Secrets* and one quote from his book *The Sacred Journey*.

ISBN
978-1-5255-7897-7 (Hardcover)
978-1-5255-7898-4 (Paperback)
978-1-5255-7899-1 (eBook)

1. RELIGION, CHRISTIAN LIFE, CALLING & VOCATION

Distributed to the trade by The Ingram Book Company

CONTENTS

Dedicated to my wife and best friend,
Robin Young Postill

ACKNOWLEDGMENTS

Special thanks to the United Church of Canada, especially Timothy Eaton Memorial Church, for supporting me as a candidate for ordained ministry when I was a longshot at best.

This memoir would never have achieved lift off without considerable assistance and encouragement from several folks for whom I am grateful. In particular, my childhood friend and chief go-to-guy John Birke helped in many ways including "sniff testing" each draft. Also, my good friend and colleague the Rev. Phil Hobbs inspired me by sharing newly-written chapters from his own heartfelt memoir.

Thanks to the FriesenPress team for their expertise, guidance, and patience. In addition, I specifically wish to express my gratitude to the Rev. Dr. Malcolm Sinclair for his affirming and validating "Foreword."

Lastly, my thanks to Robin, who helped me in ways too numerous to list. No aspect of this memoir is more important to me than the dedication page.

It is important to tell at least from time to time the secret of who we truly and fully are—even if we tell it only to ourselves—because otherwise we run the risk of losing track of who we truly and fully are and little by little come to accept instead the highly edited version which we put forth in hope that the world will find it more acceptable than the real thing.
—Frederick Buechner, *Telling Secrets*

Amazing grace! How sweet the sound,
That saved a wretch like me!
I once was lost, but now am found;
Was blind, but now I see.
—John Newton, *Amazing Grace*

My assumption is that the story of any one of us is in some measure the story of us all.
—Frederick Buechner, *The Sacred Journey*

FOREWORD

If you have stereotypes of church ministry and church ministers—you know, stodgy, precious, boring, and easily shocked—meet Gordon Postill and be surprised, enthralled, and even stunned.

The real-life adventures revealed here are more like Sampson, Ishmael, Goliath, and Elijah than some pampered High Priest with pure bloodlines and hidden motives.

Gordon is a bright mind with tremendous recall for content and affect. He is honest to the point of embarrassment, and warmly engaging to the point of friendship.

He and I have nearly crossed paths over the years, admire many of the same heroes, and share the same profession, but his adventure is in 3D, while mine seems in sepia.

This book is real, instructive, encouraging, and empowering. One wild life in the thrall and call of God.

The Rev. Dr. Malcolm Sinclair,
D.Min., D.D., M.S.M.
Minister Emeritus,
Metropolitan United Church,
Toronto, Canada

PROLOGUE

I awoke one morning in late March 1970. Terribly hung over, I couldn't recall much about the previous evening. Over the past several months, my alcoholic blackouts had become more frequent. Yet this morning was different.

I inexplicably began to honestly look at my life, something I hadn't done in ages. The result of this candid self-assessment quickly morphed into sheer torment. An insidious sense of doom, gradually seeping into my consciousness around the fringes over the past few weeks, now mercilessly bore down and enveloped me.

I knew instinctively that my clever schemes and panoply of sensual pleasures could no longer shield me from the truth. My three-year debauched, deceitful romp of endless thrills and delights was on life support. Brutal consequences were quickly heading my way. It would soon be time to pay the piper. I had been running up quite a tab. In short, I was fucked.

After miraculously passing my first year, I was now on the verge of failing a second straight year at Queen's University in Kingston, Ontario. Failing one year was bad enough; however, failing two consecutive years, especially for someone whose academic record from high school had earned him a coveted early acceptance from this renowned bastion of learning, was an entirely different kettle of fish. This kettle had the stench of a real loser. That loser was me.

Without any twinge of personal accountability or conscience, I had squandered the opportunity for a first-rate education. Having been unexpectedly abandoned several months earlier by my first real love, a pervasive heartache still shook me to the quick, leaving me emotionally paralyzed. My adolescent nemesis of feeling like a self-conscious, flawed outsider surfaced stronger than ever. I had no sense of direction and had pretty much exhausted what should have been an abundant supply of cash.

Everything was closing in on me. I felt ashamed, adrift, and afraid. My life lacked meaning. More to the point, I lacked meaning.

Feeling trapped like a wounded animal, I desperately bolted outside to get some air. Aimlessly walking around for who knows how long, I eventually found myself down by Lake Ontario where it abuts the campus.

It was a cold, overcast, and windy day, and the big ice was breaking up; chunks were flowing at a good speed, and a number of people had gathered on the shore to check out the sights. At some point without any forethought, I left the shore and soon found myself impulsively jumping from ice floe to ice floe.

As if on automatic pilot, I headed toward the fastest-moving floes about three hundred feet farther out in more open water. I lost my footing on the slippery chunks of ice several times and fell into the freezing water. Each time I struggled to climb back onto the floes, I cut my hands on the sharp edges.

Riding the blocks of ice and looking back to shore, I saw several people beckoning for my safe return. Totally unfazed and full of disdain, I defiantly kept going. I didn't give a shit whether I lived or died. After somehow making it back to shore, I had a sense of foreboding that this intimate brush with death had merely been a mild precursor of what lay ahead.

CRACKED OPEN

In October 2010, on the eve of open-heart surgery to replace my aortic valve which apparently had been defective since birth, I knew one thing for certain. Even if the operation should go fatally awry, my life had already been blessed beyond measure. Thankfully, my surgery and post-operative recovery couldn't have gone better.

Yet five months later, while attending to my longtime ministry as a hospice chaplain, I was cracked open once again, though this time not physically. A harrowing memory from forty years earlier drifted into my consciousness. I recalled perilously riding fast-moving ice floes on Lake Ontario, with no concern whatsoever for my safety. Shortly afterward, additional memories flooded in from the tormented yet ultimately transformative decade that immediately followed.

An inexplicable yearning welled up within me to truthfully write about this crucial period that, for all intents and purposes, set the table for how the rest of my life would unfold. In what felt like a deal-breaker, the players and the events from these life-defining years needed to tell their own story in their own voice and on their own terms with no holds barred. I owed them that much. To make this happen, the story must be told exclusively from the perspective of who I was at the time. Equipped with a new aortic valve, I started writing.

FLAWED

EARLY YEARS: 1948-1967

I was born on October 23, 1948 at Toronto General Hospital. While my mother was birthing me in the delivery room, my father was in the waiting room listening to Foster Hewitt provide the radio broadcast for that evening's National Hockey League game between the Toronto Maple Leafs and the Chicago Blackhawks. The Leafs won the game 6–1. I was off to a good start!

—

My dad, Lloyd Postill, was born in 1903 and raised on a small farm in the countryside just outside of Paris, Ontario, about sixty miles southwest of Toronto. Dad's parents were modest, hard-working folk who did their best to support their five children. Then tragedy unexpectedly befell the family. My dad's father was struck and instantly killed by lightning while taking shelter next to the barn during a freak and violent afternoon thunderstorm. Dad was right there when this horror happened. He was eight years old.

His mother soon moved them to town where she opened a boarding house to make ends meet. Like the rest of his siblings, Dad quit school at sixteen to bring in some extra cash and help keep the family afloat. His mother's protracted death from cancer when he was in his twenties was another rough blow for the entire family.

As he got older, my father developed a pleasant, rather superficial manner which helped him to keep things upbeat and on an even keel.

Dad always tried his best to avoid any kind of tension or conflict. Eventually he would become an excellent salesman and good paying commission jobs quickly came his way. Elegant features and a debonair style increased his appeal on all fronts. He took a fancy to fine clothes and life in the fast lane with all its trappings.

During my early years my father worked in Toronto but right around the time I became a teenager he was away a lot on business. He worked as the district manager for a large catering firm, Crawley & McCracken Co. Ltd. that had several extensive contracts with both of Canada's national railway companies. Not having a car, Dad used both the Canadian Pacific Railroad and the Canadian National Railroad to cover huge amounts of territory in northern Ontario. He knew all the railroad personnel by their first name whether they were porters or conductors.

Each winter Dad spent hours outside flooding the backyard so my sister Louise and I, along with our friends, could have some fun skating and playing hockey. Although not your typical handyman, my father even rigged some floodlights to the clothesline so that we could skate at night. He also replaced many panes of glass that errant pucks invariably shattered every year.

—

My mother, Gertrude "Nixie" Wright, was born in 1915 and raised in a fairly well-to-do family in Guelph, Ontario, about forty-five miles west of Toronto. When Mom was in her early twenties, her own mother, with whom she was quite close, died suddenly. A few years after her mother's death, Mom's father and her younger sister Hilda, both staunch Catholics, completely severed their ties with her when she dared to marry my Protestant father against their wishes. Never one to take any kind of personal affront lightly, Mom responded by firing back her own volley. She converted to Protestantism, defiantly declaring that her children would be raised as Protestants too. Classic Nixie.

None of Mom's features really stood out other than her height, or lack thereof. She was four feet eight. Nonetheless, she was indeed a force with which to be reckoned. My mother often said that she could do all the things the big girls did and do them better than most. Mom would prove this to be the case throughout her life. Woe to those who when first meeting my mother made light of her size. To my recollection, no one ever made that same mistake twice.

My mother was a no-nonsense person who found little pleasure in mundane conversations and social chit-chat. Although she didn't have much of a natural aptitude for introspection herself, she appreciated being around others who could plumb the depths of creative thought and critical discourse. Mom enjoyed poetry and often hosted monthly Pen Guild meetings where about a dozen creative writers and aspiring poets gathered to hone their craft.

She was an excellent cook and enjoyed serving sumptuous dinners on special occasions; however, it was her unique manner for displaying the meal's colorful courses along with the fine china and cutlery that truly set Mom apart from her contemporaries. Her table presentations always elicited rave and memorable reviews from fortunate guests. My mother loved to be the center of attention. She was also quite adept at making sure that this always happened, one way or another.

My mother worked as the executive secretary and office manager for an architectural firm located just down the street from our house. This made it possible for her to come home and prepare nice lunches for Louise and I during the week. No brown bag lunches for Nixie's kids. Mom consistently did her best to ensure that Louise and I were well-mannered, well-spoken, and considerate of those less fortunate.

—

Louise was four years younger than me. She was pretty, somewhat precocious, and clearly Daddy's little girl. We had a fairly normal sibling relationship with plenty of teasing and constant spats. Although we had our own group of friends, as Louise grew older, we would often battle each other in games such as Monopoly and Crazy-Eights. Being older, I won most of the time but Louise would fight right to the end.

Louise's drive and motivation were clearly evident when she took first place by beating all her grade two classmates in the annual school skating contest. About thirty kids began dashing around the perimeter of a good-sized outdoor rink but in the first turn many of them fell.

Unfazed, Louise strategically navigated her way past fallen contenders, proceeded at full speed with her arms pumping, never looked back, and easily won. As her older brother, I beamed with pride.

When Louise was ten, my mother and her teachers thought that she would benefit from some increased daily structure. Consequently, Louise became a boarder at Saint Mildred's College, a well-respected Anglican school in downtown Toronto. St. Mildred's also had an excellent reputation for its music program, and Louise was already showing considerable musical ability. She came home on most weekends but was always happiest when returning to school on Sunday afternoons.

—

Mom and Dad rarely talked about their own family histories. There was a brief period of time when Louise and I were both young that our parents would periodically take us by train to visit some of Dad's siblings in Paris for a weekend. But one night after Louise and I had gone to bed, my father and his brother Welby became falling-down drunk in front of my mother. Mom immediately put the kybosh on any further visits.

Neither Louise nor I seemed to mind. The outings themselves, exciting novelties at first, had become boring. We missed our neighborhood friends. So much for extended family and ancestral roots.

—

My childhood years growing up in Toronto seemed fairly seamless and unremarkable—at least for a while. We lived in a well-kept middle-class neighborhood about five miles northeast of downtown Toronto. I never saw people of color except when catching a movie or shooting pool downtown with my teenage chums. English was the only language I heard except for French in high school or Finnish from a family living down the street from us.

The kids I knew were primarily from Protestant families with a few Catholics in the mix. Most attended church in varying degrees. I never knowingly met a Jew until my first year at university. Each school morning commenced with everyone reciting, or at least lip-synching, the Lord's Prayer.

When I was about eight years old and playing with some friends downstairs in our house, I fell and severely chipped one of my front teeth. Our family dentist said that a crown wouldn't be possible until my late teens, when the tooth would have finally stopped growing. Adding insult to injury, shortly afterward I chipped this same tooth even more while playing hockey. As a result, I became very self-conscious, felt deeply flawed, and usually kept my lips closed when smiling.

When I was about twelve years old, my father's company relocated to Sudbury, a town about 250 miles north of Toronto. Since Dad would still be away each week regardless of where we lived, my parents decided not to leave Toronto. My father subsequently rented the spare bedroom in the home of a retired couple in downtown Sudbury and came home every other weekend.

—

Prior to grade ten, I really enjoyed my schools: Maurice Cody (kindergarten through grade seven), Hodgson Senior Public (grade eight), and Northern Secondary (grade nine). Maurice Cody was easily my favorite. I had a few close friends, especially Jimmy Birke and Robin Parke. We had a lot of fun together playing sports and games and just hanging out.

Just before I started grade ten, my mother's financial acumen enabled my parents to buy their first house in Leaside, a completely different township. Although the move itself was less than a mile, I still needed to change high schools. Thankfully, I already knew some of boys from Leaside High School after having played organized hockey with them over the past three years.

Nonetheless, this change in high schools would prove to be a huge setback for me in terms of my self-confidence and peer relationships. Like any school, Leaside had its own social dynamic. Most of my peers had already formed friendships and cliques by the time I arrived on the scene. Several of my new classmates had known each other since grade one. As an outsider, I never seemed able to gain a comfortable purchase within the school's culture. I often overcompensated for my insecurities by being arrogant and sarcastic. On more than one occasion, I was told about the huge chip on my shoulder.

—

Throughout high school my degree of self-consciousness about my missing front tooth increased tenfold. Feeling flawed, I became paralyzing inhibited around girls and lacked the necessary confidence for dating. Although sexual fantasies helped somewhat to mitigate my increasing frustration, a pervasive sense of self-loathing was developing deep roots.

Starting at the age of fourteen and over the course of the next three summers, I worked for my father's company as a cook's assistant in a large mess hall located about thirty miles outside of Sudbury. The mess hall staff provided the meals for the men who worked nearby in various nickel mines. On my weekly day off, I usually hitched a ride to Sudbury to see the sights and maybe catch a movie. Sometimes Dad and I met for lunch during these outings.

I enjoyed being away from home, yet just like in high school, I felt self-conscious. Even though these summer girls openly flirted with the new guy from the big city, my sexual rites of passage continued to stall. No wonder as a teenager The Rolling Stones breakout song "(I Can't Get No) Satisfaction" immediately become my anthem. If the old wives' tale about masturbation had been true, I'd have been completely blind by sixteen.

—

School work was always easy for me. I could complete assigned homework either immediately after class ended or just prior to class starting the next day. I took great pride in never having to take any books home except on those occasions when pulling an all-nighter to cram for exams.

The high points of my childhood and teen years were sports and games. I could more than hold my own in hockey and football, was an excellent card player (hearts, canasta, poker, and cribbage), played a very good game of chess, and shot a fair game of pool.

More and more, I noticed how my parents seemed so completely out of synch with each other, almost as though they were worlds apart. My mother often tried to engage my father in topics such as politics, literature, and current events for which she felt great passion. Dad, on the other hand, rarely responded to her entreaties, preferring instead to quietly read his newspaper or work on a crossword puzzle.

Invariably in these situations, a verbal fight ensued; however, Dad usually pre-empted their heated discourse within minutes by heading upstairs to their bedroom with his newspaper or outside for some yard work. Whenever seeing or hearing my dad vigorously raking our asphalt driveway, I instinctively knew that my parents had just had a row.

When I was about seventeen, Mom told Dad not to bother coming home anymore. My mother's ultimatum really didn't surprise me. Even as a teenager, I could easily see the unhappiness in their marriage. Quite frankly, I felt relieved by their separation. The constant tension between them had become wearisome and boring to me. By no longer coming home, Dad became an even more irrelevant footnote in my life.

—

However, after my parents separated, Mom's interest in me significantly increased. I felt suffocated by her well-meaning preoccupation with my life. The local pool hall quickly became my favorite getaway and gave me some space to breathe. None too soon, the day finally arrived for me to leave home for university.

A MOTH TO A FLAME

AN UNFETTERED UNDOING:
1967–1970

Queen's University: First Year

In early September 1967, as the train pulled out of Union Station in Toronto for the three-hour trip to Queen's University in Kingston, Ontario, I was primed for satisfaction. My severely chipped front tooth, which had left me feeling flawed and self-conscious ever since breaking it when I was eight years old, had finally been capped. I now had a great smile. Let the good times roll!

—

However, the first week at university was proving to be abysmal for me on several fronts, especially with the babes. My initial high hopes for a satisfaction-laden-life as a college student away from home certainly hadn't lasted long. Although I enjoyed my new roommate and other residence mates, that old nagging sense of feeling flawed quickly returned. I was the only one of my peers who didn't know how to drive. Most of my new chums were far more experienced with girls than I was. At least that was their story.

Moreover, being the only one who didn't drink alcohol also set me apart. In high school, I drank alcohol twice in grade thirteen but couldn't stand the taste of either liquor or beer. During the first week of orientation, I even tried fitting in with the residence culture by forcing myself to drink some beer. Not surprisingly, this exercise produced the same undesirable outcome.

Good-looking girls were everywhere. The prospect of incredible sexual romps was dizzying. Yet orientation week, especially the dances, had turned into a nightmare for me. Even when I mustered up the courage to ask someone to dance, words escaped me once the song ended. Talk about ineptitude. I was pathetic.

Most of my peers seemed socially fearless while I sucked air on the sidelines. Obviously the recent dental enhancement was not the magic bullet for curing my relational inhibitions, especially around girls. Despair seeped into my soul. In less than one week, my optimism literally vanished. I was stunned by how quickly my fortunes had plummeted since setting foot on campus. Never had I felt so disheartened.

—

On the last night of orientation week, I was playing cards with my residence mates. We were cooling our heels before heading over to the week's final and biggest dance. Everyone was psyched about the evening's prospects except for me who secretly wished our card game could last forever. Winning and feeling good about myself, I certainly wasn't in any hurry for another exercise in futility at a dance.

As my chums started to get a good buzz from their respective libations, they implored me to sample some of the rye whisky I'd bought earlier in the day at their insistence. Figuring that there was really nothing to lose, I impulsively opened my 12 oz. bottle of Black Velvet Rye Whisky and downed a huge swig. However, the taste was so awful that I gagged and barely kept from puking.

I was just on the verge of berating these assholes for having egged me on to drink that shit when the magic struck me right between my eyes. My cheeks flushed. I felt light-headed. An inner, electric surge almost jolted me out of my chair. My chums raucously laughed and applauded. Within minutes, the bottle was empty. I felt completely unfettered without a care in the world.

Waking late the next morning, I was still fully dressed and lying under a blanket on top of my bed. My throat was parched and my lips were dry. Yet otherwise I felt terrific. Although I couldn't remember much about the previous evening after we'd left for the dance, some of my mates provided me with a full account of the night's activities. Apparently when not falling down, I had danced up a storm with several coeds. Hearing this report, I felt giddy and buoyant.

For the first time in many years I didn't feel like a flawed, self-conscious outsider. A sense of belonging swept over me. Finally, I had caught up to the real me that had waited so patiently all this time to be discovered. My shackled and lonely life now seemed like a mere mirage. Enchantment beckoned. I was born again.

—

Beginning a Bachelor of Arts degree program, I registered in the usual introductory courses. These "101" weekly courses had large enrollments, typically over two hundred students; however, one of these courses in Canadian history also involved a bi-weekly seminar.

For this course's seminar component, the class was arbitrarily divided into separate groups of about twelve students. Several graduate students majoring in this field of study led those various seminar groups. These graduate students, called Teaching Assistants or TAs, also graded all of their respective students' written assignments.

I faithfully attended each course's lectures for about a month before becoming disenchanted by the seemingly meaningless content and the ever-so-boring professors. By mid-October, I stopped going to any lectures whatsoever, trusting that the other two hundred plus students in attendance would easily camouflage my absences. Yet there was no way of getting around those bi-monthly history seminars where chronic absenteeism could be easily spotted, automatically ensuring a failing grade.

—

By this time, I was getting much better at pacing my drinking and working on what Bob Seger would later famously term those "night moves." I quickly discovered how weed and hash, when combined with alcohol, could transport me to even more dizzying heights. In late October, thanks to this newfound self-confidence in a bottle, I finally got laid. A few weeks later, I awoke with a different partner. Though unaware of this at the time, I had officially jump-started my fifteen-year promiscuous romp. Life never seemed so full of promise.

Ironically, the Canadian government helped me launch my debauched lifestyle. In those days students could receive sizable low-interest loans. Moreover, depending on circumstances, several students also garnered large grants which were essentially free gifts of money with no strings attached. Since my parents were separated, the government used only Mom's income for determining my overall financial needs. I was literally in the money!

—

Surprisingly my father, albeit indirectly, also enhanced my already flush financial situation. Dad was an excellent cribbage player. When I was between the ages of ten and fifteen, he taught me to play at a high level as well. By the time I arrived at Queen's my crib game had never been better. As luck would have it, many of my floor mates in residence really liked cribbage. In fact, they enjoyed playing crib even more with some money on the line. Better still for me, they were only good players at best.

Right from the start of classes there were always a few of us playing cribbage in residence. We bet fifty cents or a dollar (that's 1967 money!) on each game, the wager doubling whenever the loser was "skunked." Playing several games a day, I rarely lost. Most of my opponents had plenty of spending money and regarded their cribbage bills as mere pocket change; furthermore, by the end of the year they had all become damn good cribbage players.

—

Alcohol magically distanced me from years of feeling insecure, lonely, and sexually inept. I desperately didn't want my new life to end. But in late November, some ominous handwriting was already on the wall. By then I had figured out that the results from the final exams in April would surely expel me from Eden unless my overall term work could provide some kind of counterweight.

To give my lackluster written assignments at least a fighting chance, I decided to pay through the nose and have them typed. Thankfully, my cribbage winnings made this possible. But even the expensive typing's impressive facelift couldn't hide my work's vacuous content. I was fortunate to escape first semester with a C– average as my grades could have easily been much worse.

In the second semester I lacked the inner resolve to turn things around and just kept churning out more meaningless, mediocre bullshit. My increasingly indulgent lifestyle expeditiously stripped me of even the most marginal sense of discipline and ambition. Nonetheless, with only one remaining major assignment before the final exam, I had miraculously maintained that precarious C– average.

—

That last assignment was a seminar presentation that I had postponed for as long as possible. In fact, with just one seminar meeting remaining before the term ended, I was one of only two students who hadn't already presented their work. Even with doomsday looming, I just couldn't summon up the will to see this grim charade through to the finish.

Being desperate, I put the word out about my willingness to buy someone else's paper. Still having considerable cash on hand, I could fortunately pay a premium price if necessary. There was just one catch: any interested sellers needed to be from other seminar groups to ensure that my group's TA wouldn't recognize the scam.

As luck would have it, someone who was low on cash approached me with an offer. She was from another group and agreed to sell me her paper for a very exacting price. How could I blame her? She knew my back was up against the wall. I quickly glanced at a copy of the paper she had just presented very favorably to her own seminar group. Everything looked fantastic: great content, well-articulated, lots of footnotes, and a considerable bibliography.

After forking over the cash and having the paper in hand, I relished my cleverness. I had the paper re-typed and arrived for the seminar without a worry in the world. Just as the seminar was about to start, the course's professor unexpectedly joined us. Apparently he had a reputation for randomly checking out his course's students as well as the seminar leaders themselves.

While waiting for the first student to finish her presentation, I whimsically considered how the professor's presence could actually be a great blessing for me. I was about to present an outstanding piece of scholarship, witnessed by my seminar group and the course's professor to boot. I felt like the cat that had just swallowed the canary.

Yet right from the get-go, the professor challenged everything I said. He became more incensed with every aspect of my paper. I felt besieged by his unanticipated and relentless assault. Knowing absolutely nothing about the subject matter itself, it was impossible for me to bullshit my way out of this avalanche of professorial chastisement. When the class finally mercifully ended, I felt like having just been drawn and quartered at the Old Bailey. Exiting "stage left" as quickly as possible, I overheard the professor and the teaching assistant verifying my name.

Although not surprised two days later when my paper received an F, I wasn't prepared to see the extent of the professor's critical comments. Red ink was everywhere. The paper's facts, footnotes, and bibliography were grossly inaccurate. Completely bewildered and seeking some answers as to how the fuck this could have happened, I tried to find the asshole who sold me the paper, but didn't know her name and couldn't remember what she looked like.

———

With exams beginning in less than a week, my prospects looked grave. Although having passed all the written assignments except for this latest seminar debacle, each course's final exam would ultimately determine my fate. Being clueless about any course's content, I was on very shaky ground at best. According to the university's policy, full time students needed to pass at least four courses during an academic year to receive credit for them. Passing only three courses or less meant diddly.

Although clearly behind the eight ball, I felt surprisingly motivated. Maybe there was still enough pride left to attempt salvaging my school year. I first needed to borrow and photocopy tons of missed lecture notes from classmates. Fortunately, I still had enough cash on hand to pay for the huge photocopying tab. I then quickly combed through all the photocopied notes to identify each course's most pertinent material.

Last but not least was the onerous chore of rewriting the most salient points. This last step was essential. High school taught me that I couldn't effectively cram content unless the material was organized and formatted in my personal style. Luckily, there were three to four days between each of my exams. This piece of scheduling good fortune would enable me to focus on one course at a time.

I also instinctively knew that the Canadian history course with the recent seminar horror show was already a lost cause and beyond saving. Even if I somehow aced that course's final exam, the professor would personally deliver the knockout blow. I therefore decided to skip that exam altogether to save valuable time and energy. Although this strategy was really a no-brainer, I couldn't help feeling more anxious knowing that now there was absolutely no margin for error.

—

Over the next two weeks, I crammed my ass off for the remaining four final exams. Everything was a frenetic blur; however, after the political science, English literature, and economics exams, I ran out of gas. I just couldn't get motivated to study for the philosophy exam. To make matters worse, I realized that there was no way to bullshit my way through syllogisms, logic, and deductive reasoning. I was fucked.

The night before the exam, I crashed about midnight, hoping for one last cramming session in the morning before the early afternoon reckoning. Yet upon waking, I could only barely open one of my eyes on account of a mammoth sty. This seemed like the final nail in my coffin until it dawned on me that this could be like a miraculous "call from the governor."

Sure enough, within minutes of entering the campus medical office, I received an official "stay of execution" with a physician's note granting me permission to write the exam later that summer. Dropping the note off at the Registrar's Office, I learned that Toronto was one of the locations where the exam would be held. I felt my sty shrinking already.

One month later, I received my official transcript. I had passed political science, English literature, and economics, albeit with the lowest grades in my life. If I passed philosophy later that summer, my first year would be astoundingly salvaged.

Harbinger

After the final exams I returned to the previous summer's construction job as a flagman. This huge project involved widening many miles of a major highway about a hundred miles north of Toronto. Like the other construction workers, I ate and slept in a large portable trailer near the construction site.

I hated the isolation and boredom flagmen endured. Just standing for at least twelve hours each day was physically demanding in its own right. Working from six in the morning until at least eight at night, there was only enough time after work for supper and a shower before crashing about ten. Yet the pay, especially with all the overtime, was terrific.

I always hitched rides to a nearby town on the weekends with lots of money in my pocket. Then I did something incredibly stupid. Just like the previous summer, the foreman immediately started to hassle me about my long hair. I had never let this jerk get to me until one fateful day about halfway through the summer.

After one of his harassing rants, I impulsively responded by unleashing a diatribe of obscenities. In less than a minute, I quit my job, threw down my flag, and left the site. Self-righteous indignation had carried the day. I was the "Man!" However, this rush of instant machismo reaped from this seeming moral victory quickly dissipated.

Bitter consequences soon followed. For the rest of the summer I lived with my mother in Toronto. I didn't have a job or any money. My social life was nil. Even so, things quickly turned from bad to worse.

—

One evening after being home for about three weeks, I joined my friends, Robin Parke and Bill Devitt, at Bill's house. Since Bill's mother was away, we made ourselves comfortable and proceeded to get drunk on the rum we had bought beforehand. The next thing I knew was waking up fully dressed at four o'clock in the morning and lying on top of my bed back at Mom's apartment. How I got there was completely beyond me. I couldn't even remember leaving Bill's house. But a full accounting of the previous evening's disturbing details soon came to light.

At about nine o'clock, for whatever reason, I had left Bill's house and walked out into the middle of the main street, directing traffic and shouting obscenities. Reports of my antics must have reached the police. Two officers promptly picked me up, checked my wallet, and noted where I lived. They proceeded to take me back to my mother's apartment, where she was hosting a lovely social gathering with several of her friends and acquaintances.

Some of the guests who were out on the balcony had a bird's-eye view of both the police car and motorcycle pulling up right in front of them. Even without blaring sirens, the flashing red lights heralded my arrival. The two police officers kept me vertical while bringing me to the front door. When my mother answered the doorbell, I stumbled forward and passed out on the living room carpet. Almost immediately, Mom fainted and fell right next to me. We were both down for the count.

Having just witnessed my mother's trauma, the officers decided not to press any charges against me. The guests assisted Mom to the sofa and helped me to bed. Then they left as quickly and discreetly as possible. The fallout from this incident was understandably severe. I felt terrible and apologized but the damage had been done.

—

When the date for the dreaded philosophy exam in late August finally arrived, it was evident that I had shamefully looked a wondrous gift horse in the mouth. Even with the extra bonus months to study, I was in no better shape than back in April. Within hours my first year would be toast. Although there was really no point in even heading downtown to write the exam, I went anyway.

Sure enough, when I turned over the page to begin the exam, my comeuppance came calling. The questions themselves didn't even make any sense to me. There were several different exams going on simultaneously in the room. I looked around and saw numerous students conscientiously hunkered down over their papers with an air of confidence and assurance. I just sat there waiting for the obligatory thirty minutes before being permitted to leave the room.

All of a sudden an officious-looking man entered the room and asked those students who were writing the Queen's philosophy exam to meet with him immediately in the hall. Along with a few other students, I then learned that the university had sent the wrong exam material. We were consequently given the option of writing the exam sometime in September or receiving the lowest possible passing grade for the course right there on the spot.

We all took the latter option and then joyously headed off to one of the student pubs to celebrate. Fucking unreal! I could hardly wait to share this incredulous turn of events back on campus, especially with my buddies, Ian Campbell, Chuck Corrigan, Fraser Gagner, and Richard Boxer.

Queen's University: Second Year

I arrived on campus a few days before classes started to secure some last-minute "digs." Unfortunately, the last remaining housing options close to the university were a few unappealing furnished rooms in private homes. To make matters worse, lodgers were never allowed to have visitors in their rooms. In other words, any "hanky-panky" needed to take place elsewhere.

At least by arriving early I could check out the first-year coeds at their final orientation dance before most of the student body returned to campus. A year ago at that time I'd discovered the transformative alchemy of alcohol, rapturously riding that pony ever since. Maybe once again I could catch lightning in a bottle.

Before leaving Toronto for Kingston I had hung out one night in Yorkville Village, Canada's version of England's notorious and fashionable Carnaby Street. While there I bought a new flashy headband and a very stylish pair of neon purple bellbottoms. This latter purchase would eventually prompt some coeds to give me the moniker "Purple Passion."

After knocking back several shots of straight rye with some chums, I snuck into the final "frosh" dance. Sporting my new Yorkville attire, I was looking good and feeling lucky. Second year was already off to a great start.

—

I awoke the next morning about eleven o'clock, still fully dressed and lying on top of my bedspread. For a few seconds it seemed like I was reliving that disastrous experience at my mother's place less than a month earlier. In my pant pocket I found the note, "Meet Helen T in the lobby of Victoria Hall at noon."

Although much of the previous night's activities eluded me, I did recall meeting a beautiful coed and having an incredible time. Although not able to remember exactly what Helen looked like, I knew the urgency of getting down to Victoria Hall before noon. Feeling sheepish, I arrived with five minutes to spare. Since it was noontime, many coeds were milling around the lobby of this brand-new women's residence.

Then in the blink of an eye, a tall beauty sensually sashayed over and kissed me fully on the mouth. Arm in arm, we waltzed over to the Student Union for some lunch. When the right moment arose, I coyly asked Helen to share her own highlights from the previous night to see if they matched mine. To my great relief, she happily filled in all the details.

Apparently, I had asked her to dance. Immediate lift off! After a few dances we'd made a quick getaway and proceeded to get better acquainted, initially in the Student Union, where I had stumbled through a few tunes on the piano, and then later in a secluded spot on the shore of nearby Lake Ontario.

Helen instantly became my sole curriculum in my second year. Playing on the Arts '71 intramural flag football team and enjoying high jinx with buddies, fun though they were, didn't come remotely close to how much I savored my times with Helen. Although I showed up for some classes and completed all the written assignments, my academic efforts were less than half-assed. I just wanted to be with her. Nothing else mattered, least of all my grades.

Early in the second semester, the residence security guards caught me one evening in Helen's dorm room. An anonymous tip from someone on her floor had been our undoing. Unfortunately, she was forced to find accommodation elsewhere. I was permanently barred from that particular residence and almost expelled from the university itself.

Gutted

When the school year ended, we stayed in Kingston. I got a job in construction and Helen worked in a downtown department store. One evening in May, I walked over to meet her so we could go out for dinner as usual. After I rang the front doorbell her landlady quickly appeared. She tersely informed me that earlier in the afternoon Helen had permanently left town without providing a forwarding address.

She then handed me a letter that Helen had left for me and abruptly shut the door. My hands shook as I opened the letter and read the crushing contents. Although she wished me well, Helen said that our relationship was going nowhere and needed to end. She also requested no further contact from me under any circumstances.

I felt as though a professional boxer had just punched me as hard as possible in the gut. I couldn't breathe. I doubled over and almost fell down. Dazed and weeping, I eventually made it back to my room, lay down on the bed, and cried myself to sleep, hoping never to awaken.

Over the next two weeks I repeatedly tried calling Helen at her parents' place in a nearby city, but someone always hung up when my voice was recognized. Growing more desperate, I considered pleading my case in person but couldn't bear the thought of a face-to-face rejection. I'd never withstand another body blow.

—

Shortly afterward, my grades arrived. My lackluster study effort for the final exams when Helen and I were still together had virtually eliminated any chance for a last-minute academic reprieve like last year. Sure enough, I had failed every course. However, news of officially failing second year paled in comparison to the acute pain of my broken heart.

I was so devastated that even old standbys such as alcohol, weed, and faceless sexual encounters barely mitigated my despair.

Then miraculously, the cavalry arrived. I discovered LSD. During my first acid trip, I stayed up all night listening to great tunes by The Rolling Stones, Led Zeppelin, Jimi Hendrix, Cream, and The Doors. Walking down to Lake Ontario at dawn, I beheld millions of flamingos landing and taking off in the shimmering glow. I wept with joy and felt intimately connected with the cosmos.

While working on construction for the rest of that summer in Kingston, "Clinical-White" and "Double-Barrel-Orange" LSD kept me sane. By transporting me to realms of ethereal beauty, acid soothed my soul. Yet when I wasn't tripping, my heart ached incessantly.

—

Though very disappointed by my grades, Mom was cautiously optimistic about my return to Queen's. She figured things could work out as long as I attended classes, studied hard, and cut back on my drinking. I didn't share my mother's hope but tried to stay open to the possibility of making some positive changes.

Queen's University: Second Year Repeated

When classes started, I dreaded seeing Helen on campus with some other guy. Such a sighting would have landed me straightaway in either the psychiatric hospital or the morgue. Fortunately, she didn't return to Queen's. Nor did I hear any news about her.

—

My initial good intentions for "turning over a new leaf" never gained a purchase. I occasionally attended classes, churned out the same mediocre written work, and paid typists top dollar to buff up my scholarship's marginal content. I lived solely for carnal delights.

Thankfully, sharing an apartment with my hilarious sidekick, Ian Campbell, engaging in comedic banter with other buddies, and playing intramural football for Arts '71 helped mitigate my deepening existential despair. Since I was usually in some form of an alcohol and drug induced altered state, the days of the week all seemed the same to me except for Sundays. That's when the bars were closed.

——

I awoke one morning in late March 1970. Terribly hung over, I couldn't recall much about the previous evening. Over the past several months, my alcoholic blackouts had become more frequent. Yet this morning was different.

I inexplicably began to honestly look at my life, something I hadn't done for ages. The results of this candid self-assessment quickly morphed into sheer torment. An insidious sense of doom, gradually seeping into my consciousness around the fringes over the past few weeks, now mercilessly bore down and enveloped me.

I knew instinctively that my clever schemes and panoply of sensual pleasures could no longer shield me from the truth. My three-year debauched, deceitful romp of endless thrills and delights was on life support. Brutal consequences were quickly heading my way. It would soon be time to pay the piper. I had been running up quite a tab. In short, I was fucked.

After having miraculously passed my first year, I was now on the verge of failing a second straight year. Failing one year was bad enough; however, failing two consecutive years, especially for someone whose academic record from high school had earned him a coveted early acceptance from this renowned bastion of learning, was an entirely different kettle of fish. This kettle had the stench of a real loser. That loser was me.

Without any twinge of personal accountability or conscience, I had squandered the opportunity for a first-rate education. Having been unexpectedly abandoned several months earlier by my first real love, a pervasive heartache still shook me to the quick, leaving me emotionally paralyzed. My adolescent nemesis of feeling like a self-conscious, flawed outsider surfaced stronger than ever. I had no sense of direction and had pretty much exhausted what should have been an abundant supply of cash.

Everything was closing in on me. I felt ashamed, adrift, and afraid. My life lacked meaning. More to the point, I lacked meaning.

Feeling trapped like a wounded animal, I desperately bolted outside to get some air. Aimlessly walking around for who knows how long, I eventually found myself down by Lake Ontario where it abuts the campus.

It was a cold, overcast, and windy day, and the big ice was breaking up. Chunks of ice were flowing at a good speed, and a number of people had gathered on the shore to check out the sights. At some point without any forethought, I left the shore and soon found myself impulsively jumping from ice floe to ice floe.

As if on automatic pilot, I headed towards the fastest moving floes about three hundred feet further out in more open water. I lost my footing on the slippery chunks of ice several times and fell into the freezing water. Each time I struggled to climb back on to the floes, I cut my hands on the sharp edges of the ice.

Riding the blocks of ice and looking back to shore, I saw several people beckoning for my safe return. Totally unfazed and full of disdain, I defiantly kept going. I didn't give a shit whether I lived or died. After somehow making it back to shore, I had a sense of foreboding that this intimate brush with death had merely been a mild precursor of what lay ahead.

—

One week before my final exams, I surprised myself by deciding not to flunk out with only a whimper. Remembering my miraculous comeback in first year, I considered that maybe an encore waited in the wings. However, unlike first year when the interval between each exam had been several days, this year's harsher schedule allotted me only one or two days.

I borrowed and photocopied vast amounts of lecture notes from colleagues yet severe time constraints prevented me from properly assessing and formatting the material. Even so, I still forged ahead and pulled all-nighters before each of my five exams, relying on years of cramming expertise to beat the steep odds.

After each exam I barely had time to recoup before plunging into another course's content. On one occasion when handing in my test materials much earlier than any of the other students, I noticed one of the proctors regarding me quite disparagingly. I couldn't resist telling her that the exam had been a piece of cake! Such bravado was short-lived.

After the last exam, I felt washed out and despondent. The tiny ray of hope that carried me through the exams had vanished. Since I had squandered my entire student grant and loan money without even paying the full tuition, no official transcript would be forthcoming. However, I really didn't need a piece of paper to find out my grades. I had just failed another year.

Exodus

I returned to my former construction job in the Kingston area and managed to get through the summer thanks to magical elixirs and less-than-magical one-night stands. Although turning my life around was starting to feel unlikely, I desperately needed to get far away from Kingston with its ghosts and wreckage. Many of my classmates, now looking like future world-beaters, would soon be returning to campus in mid-September for graduate school. Seeing them again and hearing about their exciting career aspirations would only add to my already extensive humiliation.

Although bloodied and battered, I wasn't quite ready to throw in the towel. Like a dazed boxer desperately in need of a protective standing eight-count before resuming the fight, I had to get my shit together in a place where no one from Queen's could find me. In late August, I suddenly realized that working underground as a miner in the nickel mines of northern Ontario would provide me with the perfect cover. One week later in Toronto after briefly seeing my mother and a few friends, I found myself boarding a train at Union Station just as I had done three years earlier when leaving for Queen's. Regrettably, that's where any similarity ended.

STANDING EIGHT-COUNT: 1970–1973

Arriving in Sudbury, I was still reeling. Just a little over three years ago I'd stood in an entirely different kind of line with other students to register for my first-year courses at one of the country's best universities. Now I was standing in line with a motley crew of all ages seeking employment with the International Nickel Company (INCO).

INCO was experiencing a hiring boom so there was no difficulty getting a job. Once hired I purchased several tools of the trade: steel-toed rubber boots, rubber gloves, heavy long-underwear, overalls, hardhat, and a metal lunch pail. INCO provided a battery-powered light that hooked on to the front of my hard hat.

Lunchroom Underground at Frood Mine—I'm sixth on the left,
flashing the peace sign. I've carried this photo in my wallet ever since then.

I quickly found a low-end boarding house and shared one of the several bedrooms with three other men. We ate two hot meals in a cramped communal dining room and picked up our full lunch pails when heading off to work. Those of us without transportation carpooled with others who had wheels and helped them pay for the gas.

I worked three alternating shifts: days, afternoons, and nights. Since these shifts changed weekly, maintaining a regular routine especially for sleeping, was impossible. Just as I started to settle in to one week's rhythm, each forthcoming week ushered in a completely different routine. The underground environment itself was foreboding and completely alien to me. Unrelenting dust, darkness, and danger were all part of a miner's daily grind. Though infrequent, accidents were usually serious and sometimes fatal.

—

The end of each shift always brought a palpable sense of communal relief when we crammed into a device affectionately called the "cage," which quickly carried us up half a mile to the surface. No definition truly does justice to the hybrid blend of smells emanating from thirty miners packed together in the cage like sardines with metal lunch pails between their legs. Words such as "pungent" or "rank" don't even come close to describing the aromatic assault during that two-minute ride to freedom at the end of each shift.

Filthy layers of clothing, garlic, gasoline and grease, cigarette smoke, chewing tobacco, spicy deli meats, cheeses, and good-old-fashioned sweat fiercely vied for attention. Nonetheless, those silent farts consistently took first prize, eliciting considerable grade school bathroom humor. Fortunately, this stultifying stench-fest was short-lived.

Exiting the cage and breathing freely again, we headed for the changing area known as the "dry." The hot shower taken right after working a shift underground was a primal delight. After showering and changing into street clothes, everyone quickly headed to their cars and got the hell out of there.

—

The winters in Toronto, where temperatures often dipped below zero degrees Fahrenheit, in no way prepared me for Sudbury's colder and longer winters during which block heaters were necessary to keep car engines warm enough to start. Even so, underground was much, much colder. It was impossible for me to stay warm regardless of how many layers of clothing I wore.

The air-powered drills required water to keep the various drill bits from getting stuck when penetrating the rock's surface. Although rubber gloves were absolutely necessary, they didn't provide any warmth for my hands. Guiding a heavy, heaving jackleg drill while changing drill bits ranging from two to twelve feet in size took total concentration. A loss of focus, even momentarily, could easily lead to permanent disfigurement or worse.

Like everyone else, numb hands and all, I hunkered down and did my job. Fortunately, I received plenty of excellent tutelage from some seasoned veterans who befriended me. While patiently training me, they were constantly amazed by my complete lack of those natural mechanical skills with which most guys were supposedly born.

During the first few months they good naturedly sent me off at times to search for tools such as "sky hooks" and "board stretchers." Hopelessly duped initially, I eventually became savvier about their pranks and even created some of my own in response. All in all, it was good fun. In terms of the job itself, I surprised many people, including myself. Within a year I became a fairly adept driller. My first passing grade in over three years felt especially sweet.

—

Like many miners, especially new hires, I sought a physician's assistance to help me cope with my ever-changing work schedule. Fortunately, INCO offered terrific health coverage for physician visits and prescriptions. Each medication was only thirty-five cents, and if one was hooked up with the right doctor, refills were pretty much automatic and limitless. Word of mouth informed me that Valium was particularly effective for aiding sleep.

It didn't take long for me to figure out that by doubling and eventually tripling the prescribed dosage, this medication not only solved my sleep problems but more importantly, also induced a sense of inner peace for which I hungered. Valium soon took its rightful place on my nutritional menu, alongside proven standbys: alcohol, weed, and LSD.

—

About three months after arriving in Sudbury, I found my own furnished room in a flophouse of sorts. My new place was centrally located, the rent was reasonably fair, and visitors were permitted any time day or night. The place had a certain carnival atmosphere with a fluid cast of characters usually bordering on the bizarre. There seemed to be a fairly high turnover among the fifteen or so tenants. I'm sure some of them had criminal records. We all shared two bathrooms that I used only when absolutely necessary.

Terrific bands regularly performed at dances in the city's community center and in some of the downtown bars. Laurentian University, just a few miles out of town, always had good weekend parties in its various student residences. However, I preferred the local action as the university setting painfully reminded me of my Queen's debacle.

—

One evening during that first winter in Sudbury, I took some blotter acid with a fellow miner who was a friend of my next-door neighbors. Although I didn't know him well, he seemed like a good guy, albeit a little rough around the edges. This was the kind of night to stay indoors as the temperature outside was well below zero degrees Fahrenheit. We were having a great time listening to some rock tunes on the radio in my room. The acid was powerful and carried us away to states of great bliss.

Then the radio station began to play the Vanilla Fudge tune "Season of the Witch." About midway through the song I noticed the lime green paint on my room's ceiling was swirling around and gradually turning to a dark red color. This visual effect was quite fascinating, especially when the dark red paint on the ceiling began dripping down onto the floor at the far end of my room. Suddenly, I realized that the dark red paint was blood.

Frightened, I turned to my chum for a reality check. Yet upon seeing him, I gasped and froze. He had become the most vicious and terrifying vampire I could ever imagine. His lifeless face had a grayish white pallor and he smelled like rotting meat. Extra-large front teeth, which looked more like fangs, pierced through his lower lip. Huge amounts of blood gushed freely from his mouth.

Somehow I had enough wits about me to suggest going outside to get some air. We quickly grabbed our coats and headed outside only to be met by new horrors. The streets had become rivers of blood in which enormous snakes were twisting and turning almost coming up onto the sidewalks. The evening itself was pitch black, with no cars or other pedestrians in sight. I carefully looked at my companion who was still as frightening as ever.

Without speaking, we made our way toward the closest all-night restaurant. I was freezing, scared shitless, and felt that my heart could burst at any moment. Then my companion, who had never expressed more than a very rudimentary vocabulary, asked if we were in the presence of "mystic evil." I could have died from sheer terror right there on the spot.

Unable to respond, I just kept walking. At that moment I felt more unhinged than at any other time in my life. Although I hadn't prayed or thought about God for many years, desperate times called for desperate measures. I immediately started praying the Lord's Prayer and reciting the twenty-third Psalm over and over again in my head.

After finally arriving at the restaurant, I noticed as we entered that the seated customers also looked like vampires, almost as horrifying as my companion. At my suggestion, we decided to call it a night. We walked back to the house without saying a word.

By the time I entered my room most of the drug's scary effects had significantly dissipated. I listened to some mellow tunes by The Byrds and The Moody Blues for about an hour before falling asleep exhausted. I soon moved to a better furnished room in a different part of the city and rarely saw my former neighbors.

Like those who feel the need to get right back on a horse after being bucked off, I took another hit of LSD soon after my bad trip. Everything went well but the risk, even minimal, of future horrors felt far too high. No more "Lucy in the Sky with Diamonds" mind-bending excursions for me. Thankfully alcohol, weed, and Valium proved more than capable of picking up any slack.

—

After six months of boarding the cage to start another shift underground, I could no longer deny my dire predicament. I needed to face the music and get my life back on track. Though not exactly sure what getting back on track might involve, long-term "cage time" was certainly not the answer. No one needed to tell me that without an undergraduate degree, any realistic escape from my bleak future prospects was virtually impossible.

During a meeting with the Registrar of Laurentian University in April 1971, I candidly explained what had happened at Queen's. She encouraged me to pay off the outstanding tuition as soon as possible and arrange for my transcript to be sent directly to her from Queen's. Amazing myself, I found the discipline to complete these tasks by late July.

As planned I met with the Registrar again in August. Upon seeing my grades I was totally blown away. I had actually passed all five courses, albeit by the slimmest of margins, from my last year at Queen's. Though bound to be quite challenging, I could now complete my degree in one year by successfully passing six courses with at least a "B" average. The Registrar even seemed happy for me.

—

I immediately requested a shift change to steady nights in order to attend classes. Since most miners abhorred "midnights," this shift always had a few open postings. Within less than a month my request was granted.

I enrolled in three literature courses and three religious studies courses. I chose literature as my major since most of the completed course credits from Queen's were concentrated in this area of study. Religious studies became my minor based solely on the fact that these were offered on the same days as the literature courses.

During registration I steeled myself for a daunting challenge: six courses while working full time. Yet once classes started, my initial resolve soon weakened. This bold endeavor proved much more arduous than anticipated. Things started heading south quickly.

I was eating my meals at all hours of the day and night and could barely concentrate on what was being discussed in class. Not having really concentrated in class since high school sure didn't help matters. Although Valium enabled me to sleep, upon awakening I often felt muddled and lethargic.

As the first semester progressed I felt increasingly unsettled and confused. I hadn't anticipated that my dual residency in such starkly different universes as the mines and the university would be so disorienting. Often waking up alarmingly discombobulated, I couldn't remember which universe was next on the docket.

—

I still tenaciously clung to hope, even as essays and tests loomed on the horizon. I was a fast reader with excellent short-term comprehension and retention skills. These abilities enabled me to take cramming to a whole new level whenever pulling all-nighters before exams in high school and at Queen's.

I was also an excellent bullshitter. This ability really came in handy, especially on those occasions in class when the teacher or professor asked me questions from the homework assignments which I usually hadn't done. My technique in these situations involved two essential "keys" that I honed to a true art form over the years.

Key #1 involved pouncing on the teacher's first question to the class that was even remotely associated with the minimal content I had skimmed earlier. There was an undeniable risk with this preemptive strike strategy, but one I considered well worth taking. From my perspective, merely remaining silent and inconspicuous in class always ran the much higher risk of being asked a direct question for which I had absolutely no frame of reference.

Key #2 involved the manner of my forthcoming response. Manner was critical as it could deflect possible inaccuracies in the response, thereby minimizing the teacher's suspicions about my homework compliance. I always tried to respond with a confident familiarity without ever flinching, even when taking on some serious water.

—

About the middle of my first semester at Laurentian, I found myself desperately trying to keep up with the assigned literature readings. Thomas Hardy's *The Return of the Native* had been one of several weekly assignments. Unfortunately, I only had a chance to skim the novel's first few pages on the bus ride to the university before the next class.

Dr. Edgar Wright was not only this course's professor but also the Head of the English Department. He was a refined, soft-spoken English gentleman with a dry wit. His love for teaching English literature was obvious and he was well respected by his peers and students alike. Shortly after our small class began, Dr. Wright asked how Hardy portrayed Egdon Heath at the beginning of the novel.

Given my desperate situation, I immediately pounced on this question about Egdon Heath and confidently began describing him. After about a minute, Dr. Wright calmly intervened, "That's enough, Gord." Although he proceeded to ask the same question again to my classmates, I paid little heed to what was said for the remainder of the class. I was too busy basking.

When the class ended one of my classmates, Jerry Pernu, and I went for a coffee. Although we hadn't known each other for long, a good friendship was already developing. As I started gloating about my clever performance in class, Jerry cut right to the chase. With more than a trace of self-righteousness, he emphatically pointed out that "Egdon Heath" was, in fact, a place rather than a person.

After an obscenity-laced, self-admonishing rant, I eventually regained enough composure to join Jerry in marveling at Dr. Wright's gracious response to my unmitigated bullshit. He had mercifully preempted my ridiculous over-reaching, when any further delay would have surely accentuated my ignorance and complete lack of scruples. A public humiliation on that day could very well have derailed me at a time when my hopes of completing my degree were already threadbare. During the rest of that semester, Jerry and "Egdon" (my new nickname) fondly recalled this incident

—

Around this time I decided to see my father. We hadn't seen each other in five years; however, I was now running low on cash and figured there was nothing to lose by asking for a handout. If money hadn't been an issue, I wouldn't have been seeing my dad at all. Any kind of father-son rapprochement was the furthest thing from my mind.

I figured a brief meeting in which neither one of us felt compelled to feign any personal interest for each other would be mutually desirable. To help ensure an impersonal context, I brought my friend Jerry along as a third-party buffer. My goal was to get in and get out, hopefully with funds in hand.

My father didn't initially recognize me with my long hair and headband. After we shook hands and exchanged some awkward pleasantries, Dad immediately gave me more money than I requested. However as the visit ended, he smiled and whimsically said, "Gord, life's your baby."

Leaving the office with money in hand, I felt perplexed by my father's parting comment. I'd never seen him dole out cryptic, existential food for thought. Had Dad, of all people, suddenly morphed into Kierkegaard?

—

In late December 1971, I moved in with two chums whom I'd met a few months earlier. I had decided to quit my job at INCO in mid-January. Working full-time in the mines and trying to successfully complete my degree was too overwhelming. I hoped that the reduced rent, along with the eventual unemployment insurance checks, would cover my living expenses, thereby freeing me to focus solely on my studies.

Anything less than a complete commitment to my courses would make graduation impossible. I had lost too much ground during the first semester and really needed to improve my grades down the home stretch. Nothing was more important.

Just two days before quitting my job, I was out at the university with my new flat mates. The thought of leaving the mines forever was exhilarating. Tuning up for a good residence party, we drank a few beers and smoked some great weed. Since the Super Bowl was the next day, we spontaneously started playing football on a frozen field next to one of the university's residences.

We were so high that an actual football wasn't needed for our gridiron antics. Calling out play-by-play commentaries, we took turns running with the "ball" and tackling each other. This was our own Super Bowl and we were the stars! We were having a fantastic time until I tackled one of my chums, causing us both to slide off the icy field and fall about three feet into a ditch. As we toppled head over heels, my two-hundred-pound friend fell on top of me.

A resounding crack heard by all of us was immediately followed by waves of the worst pain I could ever imagine. My right leg was shattered. As I drifted in and out of consciousness, my friends quickly carried me to a nearby dorm and called an ambulance.

At the hospital, I was diagnosed with a spiral break. Both the tibia and fibula of my right leg were badly fractured. Surgery was scheduled for early the next morning. Waking up after the procedure, I couldn't recall much after my arrival at the hospital. A full-length cast ran from my toes to upper thigh. Thank goodness for Demerol, a great surgeon, and terrific nurses.

Although planning to quit my job two days later, I was still an INCO employee at the time of the accident. This crucial fact meant that I could receive the company's very generous compensation package for any of their employees injured off the job. Although breaking a leg is never a good thing, if it had to happen, this accident could not have come at a better time.

I missed about two weeks of classes before returning on crutches. Jerry picked me up at my front door in his prized black Cougar, drove me to classes, and brought me back home, usually after we'd put away a few cold ones along with some tokes for good measure. In fact, Jerry's name should have been on my diploma too. Without his support and friendship, I would never have graduated.

I received plenty of affectionate attention from several coeds. My professors cut me considerable slack. Even on crutches, I had still landed on my feet. I passed all my courses with a little room to spare.

—

Mom and Dad, who hadn't seen each other in several years, attended my graduation. We all savored the occasion, knowing all too well that this day may never have come at all. That being said, my graduation photo, taken after I had smoked some great weed, shows me about thirty pounds overweight and vacantly gazing off to who knows where.

My leg took a long time to heal as I was drinking to excess. After finally having the cast removed, I still needed extensive rehab before being deemed ready for returning to work. All in all, I was off work for over ten months. After returning to the mines for a few months, I quit and moved back to Toronto in June 1973. Although I was certainly glad to be leaving Sudbury, the standing eight-count had kept me alive. I also had an undergraduate degree to boot.

IGNOMINY: 1973–1976

I felt great being back in Toronto and hanging out with old friends. Shortly after my return, I finished my last prescription for Valium. No longer having the great drug insurance perk from INCO, I didn't seek any additional refills. I never considered that stopping "cold turkey," even after having regularly exceeded the prescribed dosage for almost three years, could pose a problem.

I also figured that this would be a good time to quit drinking alcohol. My hangovers and blackouts were beginning to frighten me; moreover, I wanted to get in better shape for the big city's pulsating singles' scene. A few days passed uneventfully without any alcohol or Valium. Readily available weed certainly helped me with this transition.

However one afternoon while playing poker with friends, my hands suddenly began to shake uncontrollably. I couldn't shuffle or deal the cards. Initially finding my situation humorous, I soon started perspiring profusely and couldn't retain any thoughts in my head. Feeling afraid, I asked my friends for help.

We all figured that I was going through some form of alcoholic withdrawal and needed immediate professional assistance. We never even considered that some of my withdrawal symptoms could be related to Valium. One of my friends remembered having seen an alcohol and drug rehab center in downtown Toronto. We all piled into a car and within hours I was admitted to the Addiction Research Foundation as a residential patient.

—

Over a four-week period I underwent an extensive assessment process and participated in both individual and group therapy sessions. The staff quickly assessed that I already had strong alcoholic tendencies and was well on my way to becoming a full-blown alcoholic. They repeatedly emphasized that by continuing to drink alcohol, regardless of the amount, I would soon reach that stage from where very few alcoholics ever recover.

I was very candid with the staff and other patients about my use of alcohol, weed, and LSD, but I intentionally minimized my use of Valium. Living for a month with hardened heroin addicts and alcoholics, I didn't want to be singled out as the wimp who couldn't handle a benign tranquilizer. I paid dearly for my lack of candor.

By misleading the staff, I prevented them from more effectively treating my terrifying Valium withdrawal symptoms. To make matters even worse, one of the facility's nurses recognized me from Queen's where I had briefly dated her roommate. Words weren't necessary to express what we both were thinking. "Purple Passion" had lost his luster and become a drunk.

Prior to completing the residential component of the rehab program, I learned about the drug Antabuse. Apparently, anyone who drank alcohol within a thirty-day period after ingesting this drug became very sick. A brief video showed me in no uncertain terms the truth to such a claim.

In this very graphic educational video, an alcoholic took Antabuse and then willingly drank some alcohol. Shortly afterward, he became violently ill. I didn't need any additional convincing.

Wanting to stay sober, I took my first "shot" of Antabuse. The rehab staff strongly encouraged daily attendance at Alcoholics Anonymous (AA) meetings held in various settings throughout the city. Monthly doses of Antabuse dispensed at the clinic were also highly advised to help ensure my ongoing sobriety.

Rejoining my friends, I fully intended to turn over a new leaf by totally complying with all of the clinic's recommendations. Yet two AA meetings were all I could handle. Even though most of the attendees couldn't say enough good things about the program, the whole concept of introducing yourself as an "alcoholic" just didn't feel right to me.

I never attended another AA meeting. Even so, thanks to the Antabuse horror flick, alcohol didn't touched my lips for a month. However as soon as that month ended, I wasted little time before plunging back into my familiar reckless lifestyle, albeit without Valium.

—

When my unemployment benefits were close to ending, getting a job became urgent. I tried my hand at inside sales for a national aluminum company but soon hated the position and quit after six months. Even less satisfying was my short stint as an employment consultant/headhunter.

Having now become such a poor employment risk, the best of my remaining job options was work as a security guard. My first assignment was near the Toronto waterfront area in a large tannery. Before reporting for duty, I needed to get my hair cut and wear a uniform including a ridiculous hat.

I worked twelve-hour shifts beginning at eight in the evening. The smell in the tannery was so pungent that it could really take your breath away. Only after several weeks was I able to make it through an entire shift without gagging.

The guard on duty needed to walk through the entire plant every hour as part of a security check. To ensure that these rounds were being done properly, the guard needed to insert a key into various time clocks situated in every section of the plant. These clocks recorded the exact times each security round was made.

Since this patrol aspect of the job only took about thirty minutes, I used my free time each hour to read some of the classics by Dickens, Tolstoy, Hardy, and Eliot. I thoroughly enjoyed these novels, especially after having only skimmed them as a student at Queen's and Laurentian.

Most of all, I liked the fact that none of my friends or former colleagues would ever see me on the job. Like the mines, this posting was a great place to hide. Unfortunately, I was reassigned a few months later when my employer's contract with the tannery wasn't renewed. I wasn't quite as lucky in terms of visibility and privacy at my next security assignment in the main Toronto office of a national oil company.

—

My twelve-hour shifts started at seven rather than eight in the evening. Several well-dressed company executives were invariably still working when my shift started. In their midst, I felt very self-conscious dressed in my security outfit and looking like an organ grinder. Even worse, I had been required to get an extra short haircut for this position.

When starting my shift each evening, I prayed that no one from my past would see me. During my first two months, I always tried to be as inconspicuous as possible at the beginning of each shift until everyone left. Then one evening while sitting at the front desk in the lobby, to my horror I heard someone call me by name.

I quickly turned around and saw Chuck Corrigan who had been one of my closest chums at Queen's. He looked great in a three-piece suit with an eye-catching shirt and tie. You didn't need to be a rocket scientist to readily see our diametrically opposed tenure tracks.

During our brief chat, which seemed like an eternity for me, I experienced a kind of "death by a thousand cuts," with no nickel mines in which to hide. Apparently after successfully completing his undergraduate degree, Chuck had gone on to complete a Master of Business Administration (MBA). From my vantage point, Chuck looked like he had just popped out of a glossy brochure displaying members of this oil company's administrative team.

Thankfully, I believe Chuck sensed my humiliation and made a gracious exit, thereby saving me from any further embarrassment. As quickly as he made his exit, I too made mine. I quit my job at the end of the shift with absolutely no future prospects other than unemployment.

—

During the spring of 1975 any remaining remnants of my moral decency and self-esteem had pretty well checked out. I was unemployed, drinking more than ever, and living with my mother in Toronto. Mom really didn't know how to relate to this dissipated doppelganger who over time had ruthlessly stolen her son along with her dreams for him.

A summer's night proved calamitous for both of us. I was arrested in a seedy bar in downtown Toronto while drinking with two men and a woman. I barely knew the men who were about my age and had never met the woman who was probably fifteen years older than the rest of us. We were all down on our luck and doing our best to get hammered.

At some point without thinking, I impulsively reached down and took the woman's purse when she wasn't looking. Both men saw me do this. One of them joined me in the men's room where we had a grand old time rummaging through its contents. Aside from about $40 and some lipstick, there wasn't much there.

All of a sudden, the bar's owner appeared and started yelling at us. Two police officers soon arrived. Apparently, the other man at our table had alerted the woman about her missing purse. She then notified the manager who immediately called the police. I really didn't grasp the seriousness of the situation nor did the guy with me. We both started laughing and dismissed everything as a harmless joke; however, the police didn't see things that way.

Within minutes we were handcuffed, shoved in a cruiser, and taken to the nearest jail. During the trip my fellow accomplice and I made the grave error of mouthing off to the officers by calling them "pigs" and mocking them for not having more important law enforcement duties to which to attend. After we'd been charged with "theft under $200," booked, finger-printed, had our "mug shots" taken, and been placed in a cell, it was "pay-back time" for our ill-timed, disrespectful antics.

We were both beaten with short rubber clubs and received numerous hard, open-handed slaps to our faces. We sobered up real fast, knowing some serious shit was going down. At about three o'clock in the morning, each of us was allowed to make one phone call to someone who could post bail. My cellmate called one of his friends. I didn't know who to call other than my mother.

I shall never forget her quivering voice when told that she needed to bail her son out of jail for having stolen a woman's purse. As much as the sound of Mom's heartbreak over the phone cut me to the quick, it was nothing compared to her demeanor when she arrived in a taxi to post bail. My mother's whole body shook all the way home in the cab. Her faint whimpering reminded me of a small, wounded animal.

I cried, repeatedly apologized, and promised to stop drinking. But my mother never responded or even looked at me. She just kept rolling rosary beads in her little hands while her entire body spastically heaved and jerked. Once we got home, Mom immediately went to her room and shut the door. I vaguely remember going to my room and lying on top of the bed.

Staring at the ceiling for what seemed like an eternity, I struggled to accept what had just happened and who I had become. I was ashamed, lost, and numb. Most of all, I felt afraid. If there had been a gun on the bed, I would have shot myself, ending things before they got any worse.

The next morning my mother hardly acknowledged me. After breakfast she returned to her bedroom where I could hear her sobbing. Early in the afternoon while I was out for a long walk, Mom unbeknownst to me called a detective, the husband of a woman she knew socially, and told him what had happened. He was waiting for me in my mother's kitchen when I returned.

After sternly admonishing me, he said that I needed to contact a lawyer from Legal Aid for assistance. He strongly advised me not to communicate with anyone with whom I'd been drinking and not to return to that bar. He also said that without a criminal record, I'd be initially found guilty of theft under $200. Apparently by staying out of trouble with the law for the next two years I would receive an absolute discharge, and the record of this felony would be completely purged from the judicial records.

Before leaving he stressed that if this kind of situation ever happened again, I'd go to jail and be marked as a felon for the rest of my life. He also made it clear as to the horrors a person like me, young and incarcerated for the first time, could expect in jail. He didn't need to elaborate. I got the message. On December 10, 1975, in the Municipality of Metropolitan Toronto in the Judicial District of York, everything thankfully played out just as the detective had foretold.

—

Soon I started pulling security guard duty again and found another forgettable furnished room. The fear of potential jail time and its consequences tempered my reckless behavior. Yet the relationship between Mom and I remained barely intact. Even prior to this latest egregious incident, my behavior over the past eight years had already exacted a heavy toll on her.

METAMORPHOSIS

CALLED TO MINISTRY: 1976-1977

In early 1976 I learned from my good chum, Dave Smith, who was also a chartered accountant, about a new and innovative business program at the University of Windsor, Ontario. This program was specifically designed for students with a Bachelor of Arts degree who now wished to pursue a career in business. The university allowed these students to apply their non-business undergraduate course credits toward a Bachelor of Commerce degree. Once this degree was completed, students could enroll in a Master of Business Administration degree program.

This comprehensive and accelerated program entailed an extra high course load taken over two full calendar years with no breaks between various semesters. Students who successfully completed the program would have two excellent business degrees, paving the way for a rewarding career in such fields as accounting, finance, and marketing. Best of all, this program's graduates were well assured of finding gainful employment with appealing advancement opportunities.

Although not really interested in a business career for the long haul, I knew this program could get me back on my feet until I eventually discerned my true calling, if indeed there really was one. With that kind of incentive, I applied to the program and was quickly accepted. The university even sweetened the deal by providing terrific student loans to help boost the program's enrollment.

I found another forgettable furnished room close to campus and began my studies during the spring semester of 1976. Toning down my carousing, I received excellent grades in the spring and summer semesters. In fact, many of my classmates sought me out for assistance with the assignments. Maybe a lifelong career in business wasn't as far-fetched as I initially thought.

—

One October afternoon, I returned to my digs after a very important mid-term cost accounting exam. After cramming all night, I aced the test. But in spite of excelling academically, I was starting to find the program tedious and arid. The rigors from preparing for and writing this exam left me feeling ragged, tired, and depleted. Too wired to sleep, I felt like reading something completely unrelated to business.

The program's textbooks were the only books on hand except for an old Bible from my Sunday school class of 1958. How this particular Bible, or any Bible for that matter, could have still been in my possession was beyond me. During countless moves over the years, I had never noticed a Bible among my belongings. I hadn't attended church for over a decade and definitely didn't hold traditional religion in any esteem.

Nonetheless, here I was holding this Sunday school Bible from my childhood. Having a love for classical literature, I had always appreciated allegorical expression. Looking at the Bible, I remembered that "The Revelation to John" in particular was noted for this kind of literary style. Without one iota of conscious spiritual yearning, I opened the Bible to this section, hoping for some much-needed literary relief.

—

I started reading chapter one, and within seconds my fatigue and sense of emptiness lessened. With eyes riveted to the page, I beheld the words:

> ......and from Jesus Christ the faithful witness, the first-born of the dead, and the ruler of kings of the earth. To him who loves us and has freed us from our sins by his blood and made us a kingdom, priests to his God and Father, to him be glory and dominion for ever and ever. Amen. Behold he is coming with the clouds, and every eye will see him, everyone who pierced him; and

all tribes of the earth will wail on account of him. Even so. Amen. "I am the Alpha and the Omega," says the Lord God, who is and who was and who is to come, the Almighty.

Revelation 1:5–8

Feeling awed and buoyant, I sensed my eyes welling up while reading the following words:

Then I turned to see the voice that was speaking to me, and on turning I saw seven golden lampstands, and in the midst of the lampstands one like a son of man, clothed with a long robe and a golden girdle round his breast; his head and his hair were white as white wool, white as snow; his eyes were like a flame of fire, his feet were like burnished bronze, refined as in a furnace, and his voice was like the sound of many waters; in his right hand he held seven stars, from his mouth issued a sharp two-edge sword, and his face was like the sun shining in full strength. When I saw him I fell at his feet as though dead. But he laid his right hand upon me, saying, 'Fear not, I am the first and the last, and the living one; I died and behold I am alive for evermore, and I have the keys of Death and Hades....."

Revelation 1:12–18

Gobsmacked, I was suddenly swept to the floor by what seemed like a huge wave. I found myself on my knees, enveloped by joy and wonder, weeping. Never had I felt so cherished, understood, and whole. Into my consciousness burst the imperative: "Follow me. Become a minister." Though having been a non-churchgoer since my mid-teens, to me this astonishing experience felt like a "call to ministry" directly from Jesus Christ.

With absolutely nothing to lose, I decided to pursue this calling. The next day I quit the business program despite having some of the highest grades in my class. Once again, I was quitting something. Yet this time everything felt different.

—

The next day I showed up unexpectedly at my mother's house in Toronto and informed her about having quit the business program. Mom was quite disappointed by this news given the fact that I had been doing so well; however, when I told her about having been called by Jesus Christ to be a minister, she was shocked at first, and then quickly became highly indignant.

In her eyes, my irresponsible antics and overall lack of propriety over the years had been a constant source of disgrace and embarrassment to her. In Mom's view, what I was now proposing to do was even more egregious. I would be disgracing Jesus Christ and the church. Moreover, my friends found my calling absurd and even pitiful.

I couldn't really take issue with any of these reactions, as my own feelings in many ways were quite similar. Yet this inexplicable call to ministry as a disciple of Jesus Christ continued to vibrantly resonate within me. With no future prospects other than a security guard detail, I resolved to give this "call to ministry business" due process, at least for now.

—

I had no idea how Protestant denominations differed from each other. The United Church of Canada, the only denomination with which I had any familiarity—albeit from my childhood and early teen years—seemed like the best place to start. Since there were United Church seminaries in several cities throughout the country, Emmanuel College in downtown Toronto seemed like the most sensible choice. Trying to pursue my calling would be strange enough. Hopefully, home field advantage would prove helpful along the way.

After learning that the school year for the three-year Master of Divinity degree program had started one month earlier, next September seemed like the most logical time to start seminary. The intervening months would provide me with some breathing room to begin the academic application process and, even more importantly, find a United

Church congregation to endorse my candidacy. However given my track record and lack of church involvement, it wasn't inconceivable that congregations could very well decide I was unsuitable for any consideration as a ministerial candidate.

—

Once again I suited up as a security guard. Thankfully, I garnered the perfect assignment at the entrance to an Eastern European diplomatic embassy on a quiet side street in the affluent residential area just west of Avenue Road and St. Clair. By working twelve-hour shifts starting at eight o'clock in the evening, the likelihood of running into anyone who knew me was next to nil!

I also lucked out by finding a great furnished room close to my new security posting. The rent was higher than I wanted to pay but the upside was huge. Located in a stately house on Russell Hill Road, the room itself was a huge upgrade from those innumerable dumps with which I had become far too familiar in past years.

Shortly afterward, my friend Dave noticed that a nearby health club had recently opened and was offering discounted memberships for a limited period of time. The club was also coed! With those kinds of incentives, we both joined. An extensive complimentary fitness test clearly showed the poor results we had anticipated. Yet by faithfully sticking to the rigorous fitness regimen designed by the club, in less than a year we were in top shape. Despite having so many personal deficiencies, I was at least physically fit and looking good.

—

In April 1977, Emmanuel College officially accepted me into the Master of Divinity program commencing in September. But my euphoria was short-lived. The dreaded "congregational endorsement project" could no longer be postponed. Leaside United, my childhood church, seemed like the best place to start this quest. However, I just didn't want anyone from that neighborhood to know of my many fuck-ups since high school.

I felt stuck, not knowing where to turn. Then one morning in late May, a far-fetched idea came to mind. For the past several months while walking to and from work, I'd passed by Timothy Eaton Memorial Church. This truly magnificent-looking edifice just happened to be around the corner from where I lived.

One time I had actually stepped on the church's plush front lawn to get a closer look at the tastefully appointed sign listing the names of its clergy, worship times, and sermon titles for that particular Sunday. Perhaps this church with all its resources would know of some small, out-of-the-way congregation that might take a chance on a reprobate like me. There was really nothing to lose by giving this idea a try. At best the phone call could help me. At worst I could be abruptly dismissed.

One morning I decided to reach out. A man answered and politely listened while I clumsily explained the reason for my call. I was completely taken aback by his reply. He surprisingly offered to meet with me, even suggesting later that afternoon if I had the time. Though stunned by this turn of events, I readily agreed to meet with him later that day. He instructed me to use the office entrance and to inform the secretary that Dr. Morrison was expecting me.

—

Upon meeting Dr. Morrison in his study, I was amazed to learn that he was none other than the church's senior minister. I later learned that only on rare occasions did he personally field an outside call. Thankfully, mine had been one of them. Once the initial shock of actually meeting with the senior minister of Timothy Eaton Memorial Church wore off, I became more comfortable in sharing some aspects about my life.

Although I didn't elaborate too much on the past decade's darker themes and unconscionable behavior, my gut instinct told me that Dr. Morrison didn't need the fine print to grasp the bigger picture. I found him to be very compassionate and sensed that he genuinely cared about me. A week later, I met with Dr. Morrison and the congregation's two associate ministers, the Rev. Charles "Charlie" Plaskett and the Rev. Stephen Mabee. I felt at ease in this meeting as well.

—

Shortly thereafter, Dr. Morrison informed me that among other things, each "Session" within a United Church of Canada congregation was responsible for that particular congregation's spiritual oversight. To my jaw-dropping surprise, he then told me that Timothy Eaton Memorial Church was actually considering me as its own candidate for ministry. To get this process started, Dr. Morrison had arranged for me to meet with some Session members so they too could learn more about me and my call to ministry.

During that meeting a few days later, the Session members all struck me as kind and affirming, even as I shared about those years after high school when my life so quickly went off the rails. The meeting was going along quite smoothly until one of the members asked me some very pointed questions.

He asked me in a polite yet direct way how this congregation, or any congregation for that matter, could take my candidacy seriously. He hadn't heard anything in my track record that indicated some sense of responsibility or discipline. He wanted to know what I'd do next when this highly suspect venture didn't pan out.

Before answering the Session member's perfectly targeted questions, I felt compelled to inwardly address some daunting questions of my own. Was this call to ministry business merely another disillusioned sham? Even more to the point, was I a sham?

In that moment, part of me wanted to tell everyone that this calling of mine had really been a great mistake and I was sorry for having wasted their time; however, a guiding clarity quickly enveloped me. The valid concerns just expressed in this meeting had needed to be voiced for everyone's sake, especially my own. I felt a gentle shifting deep within me. Silently and resolutely, I said "yes" to Jesus and my call to Christian ministry.

I wanted to respond as openly and honestly as possible. Trusting my calling, I laid everything on the line. I admitted there was nothing about my background or character that could allay the understandable concerns that had just been expressed. Regarding the legitimacy of my candidacy for ministry, I described myself as a longshot at best.

Then without any undo defensiveness, I respectfully asked the Session members to support my candidacy in spite of their genuine concerns. After leaving the room, I found some solace in having been as transparent and honest as possible. The next step was out of my hands.

About an hour later, I was invited back to the meeting. Fittingly, the same person who had asked me the tough questions announced the group's unanimous decision to support me. They would be recommending me as an official candidate for the ordained ministry from Timothy Eaton Memorial Church to the entire Session at their regularly scheduled meeting the following week.

I went to work that evening feeling exhilarated, awed, and humbled. Since I worked alone outside at the consulate's entrance, no one saw my tears of gratitude. Throughout that night, many tears were shed.

Dr. Morrison called me the following week and offered his congratulations. The Session had unanimously approved my candidacy. He also told me that I would soon learn about my first official congregational assignment before classes started at Emmanuel. Soon afterward, all of the church staff asked me to call them by their first names. I felt comfortable doing this but could never bring myself to refer to Dr. Morrison as "George." He would always be Dr. Morrison to me.

—

About mid-August, I realized the need for a different job that wouldn't take up as much time. My Sudbury experience taught me all too well that working all night prior to taking classes wasn't sustainable, even with the best of intentions. A serendipitous encounter at four o'clock one morning solved my dilemma.

I had recently noticed a different person delivering the morning newspapers to the houses across the street from my security post. On this particular morning, I asked this person about the whereabouts of the regular carrier. She told me that the previous carrier had abruptly quit. As the home delivery manager for the *Toronto Globe and Mail* morning newspaper in this area, she was just filling in until a new carrier could be found. I expressed a possible interest in the job and told her about my upcoming school plans. We met later that morning after my shift ended and discussed the details.

This opportunity seemed tailor-made for me. The job was seven days a week and involved the delivery of about 330 newspapers. The entire paper route was close to where I lived. The newspapers had three separate drop points, each of which contained slightly over one hundred papers. Most of the route involved high-rise apartment buildings, making the deliveries much easier and quicker.

The newspapers could be picked up any time after four o'clock in the morning but needed to be delivered by six o'clock. The customers paid their accounts directly to the newspaper office, thereby relieving the carriers from this onerous task. Apparently, the previous carrier always completed his route in less than ninety minutes.

Having seen him in action, I knew the task was doable in even less time once the route became familiar to me. Allowing for the ten-minute walk to and from the initial drop point, I could get up at four and be home by six. The weekly remuneration for a route this size was far better than I anticipated. After factoring in the holiday tip tradition, I happily accepted the job.

I quit my security detail at the end of August and immediately began my newspaper delivery career. After some quick on-the-job training, I had the route down pat a week before classes started at Emmanuel. However, getting out of bed at four o'clock each morning was bound to take extra willpower, especially after a previous night's carousing. Nonetheless, I felt confident. This job could work out well, at least for a few months until those marvelous holiday tips had been safely secured. Fortunately, I had stashed away some modest savings that could tide me over for a while should the paper route become too exacting.

—

Two days before beginning my divinity studies, Stephen Mabee informed me of my first official church assignment. I was going to be the new Sunday school teacher for eleven-year-old boys. We scheduled a meeting for the following week to bring me, a teaching neophyte, up to speed. In less than six months—and in what seemed like warp speed—I had become a newspaper boy, a Sunday school teacher, a seminary student, and a candidate for the ordained ministry from Timothy Eaton Memorial Church no less. The Rubicon was now behind me.

GAME ON: 1977–1980

Emmanuel College: First Year

On that first morning at Emmanuel, I joined my new seminary class-mates in a large room where we were welcomed by some of the faculty. There were about forty-five students ranging in ages from early twenties to early sixties. About one-third of the group was female. At some point, we were asked to introduce ourselves and briefly share what brought us to Emmanuel.

Listening to my classmates' remarks, I didn't get a sense that any of them had ever failed a school year, pulled any shifts as a miner or a secu-rity guard, spent any time in a jail cell, or taken an LSD flight. When my turn came, I was briefer than most and certainly the vaguest; however, a few heads turned toward me when I mentioned that Timothy Eaton Memorial was my home church.

—

Thank goodness we took a break after two hours. I needed a stiff drink but settled for a smoke. I couldn't help wondering, *what the fuck am I doing here?* Then out of the blue I heard someone say, "I sure never expected to see Gord Postill of all people here today!" Turning around, I didn't recognize the pretty woman who had just called me by name. Seeing my bewilderment, she immediately introduced herself and explained our connection.

It turned out that Linda and I had dated a couple of times near the end of my third year at Queen's. She was looking great, and thoughts of another date quickly entered my mind. Yet within seconds this hope was dashed when Linda said she was happily married. She had been teaching high school for the past six years and was taking a few religious studies courses for her own interest.

Linda couldn't get over the fact that I was a candidate for ordained ministry. We met later for lunch and shared more about ourselves. During lunch, Linda also went on to tell me about her good friend, Helen P. Apparently Helen was taking a one-year leave from her high school teaching position to complete a Master of Arts degree right here at the University of Toronto. At Linda's insistence, I agreed to meet her and Helen for lunch the following week.

—

During that first week of classes, I felt totally like a fish out of water. Many of my classmates were quite adept at discussing biblical hermeneutics, systematic theology, and inclusive language—all topics in which I was clueless. A few of my classmates even held part-time preaching positions on weekends at rural churches.

More than anything else, one undeniable fact separated me from the rest of my peers. Unlike me, everyone had already experienced considerable church involvement prior to arriving at Emmanuel. Without one iota of my peers' formidable church pedigree, I was making my first foray into congregational life as none other than a rookie Sunday school teacher.

—

In that first week, I also met with Stephen Mabee, who showed me the curriculum and lesson plans for my Sunday school class. He was very supportive and seemed to sense my anxiety about this daunting task. Stephen encouraged me to find my own teaching style and to keep in mind that the attention span for boys of that age would be minimal at best. He encouraged me to shape the lesson content in ways that helped the boys to learn and also have some fun. Stephen's pearls of wisdom and empathy gave me some much-needed confidence. Nonetheless, I still planned a low-key Saturday night prior to entering the lion's den on Sunday.

As things turned out, my inaugural Sunday school teaching experience far exceeded my hope of merely surviving. There were about fifteen young boys with energy to burn. They seemed to like me. Some of them thought that I looked like a "dude," a reference that felt quite okay with me.

The official lesson plan for that Sunday involved important biblical characters from the Old Testament. Though loosely sticking with that topic, the overall lesson plan pretty much went out the window right from the get-go. Remembering Stephen's advice about trying to find some common ground with the boys, I went with the flow.

Since the National Hockey League (NHL) would soon begin a new season, the boys seemed bent on choosing their own hockey team's starting line-up from people in the Bible. The class was completely won over when I not only agreed with their new lesson plan but offered to join in as well. After vigorously debating our own selections, we finally came to a consensus for an all-star team.

I found the boys' energy to be quite contagious. Their knowledge of the biblical characters was much greater than mine. I was sorry when this first class ended, and I sensed that the boys felt similarly.

Over the next several months, we would always share Sunday mornings in the same mutually rewarding give-and-take manner. Even when nursing a terrible hangover from a previous evening's excesses, I still appreciated their raw energy, enthusiasm, and creativity. These boys quickly became my lads.

—

The following week, I had lunch as planned with Linda and Helen P. My attention quickly turned to Helen, who along with good looks, had a dramatic, vivacious manner. Before going our separate ways after lunch, I got her phone number. Although we agreed to get together in a week for a coffee, I called her later that same night. After a delightful conversation, we decided to meet a few days later for an evening at a popular downtown club. I could hardly wait.

Meeting at the club, Helen's magnetic energy readily appealed to me as we listened to each other's respective stories. She had a great love of English literature and planned to use the poem "The Lady of Shallot" for her Master's thesis. Helen was particularly interested in my call to ministry, which had led me to Emmanuel.

Ironically, her father, also named Gordon, was a United Church minister. After returning to her apartment later in the evening, we joyously became better acquainted. Although I hated to leave the next morning at three-thirty to deliver the newspapers, no words were needed to express how we already felt about each other.

—

An old incident from Queen's unexpectedly surfaced within the first month of our relationship and almost derailed us. Although Helen and I had both been at Queen's in 1967–70, we couldn't recall ever meeting each other. I had just been describing the disastrous seminar presentation from my first year and the ensuing professorial dressing-down, and when I finished, Helen remembered selling me her paper for my seminar presentation.

She then proceeded to describe how she had intentionally altered her paper, for which she'd received an A, before selling it to me. Appalled that I was going to pass off someone else's work as my own, she had decided to sabotage me. By radically changing the content of her original paper, Helen ensured that "my" work was filled with glaring and outlandish errors. She still relished her ploy, in spite of the dire consequences that subsequently befell me.

My initial astonishment quickly turned to outrage, and a fierce condemnatory debate ensued, putting our budding relationship in considerable jeopardy. Fortunately, cooler heads prevailed once we realized that neither one of us could justifiably claim any moral high ground. My fraudulent practice of buying someone else's work and then submitting it as mine was morally indefensible. Helen came to realize that her own actions were morally flawed by maliciously misrepresenting the product of our transaction.

This was the first real test of our relationship. Mercifully, once the mutual accusatory tone of the moment passed, we marveled at our paths once again intersecting after such a duplicitous debut several years earlier. We were also well on our way to falling in love.

—

During that first semester, I never missed a class and completed all my own assignments. I was tempted at times to buy the occasional essay, but with future ministers as classmates, such nefarious transactions just didn't seem plausible. However within two months, navigating that first semester became increasingly more difficult.

I spent most of my free time with Helen as we continued to thoroughly enjoy each other's company. Wine and a few tokes, with me having the lion's share on both counts, were usually part of each night's ritual back at her apartment. Unfortunately, by staying at Helen's most nights, I now needed to get up even earlier each morning to bike the extra four miles to pick up my first batch of papers.

—

With each passing week, I became more aware of the growing gap between my classmates' comfort level with the course material and my own. An Old Testament assignment for the book of Ecclesiastes perfectly embodied how out-to-lunch I felt as a seminarian. Although I struggled throughout the first semester with all my homework, this particular assignment proved even more arduous. None of the questions seemed logically related to the biblical material itself. Persevering as best I could, my answers were forced and even absurd.

When the professor returned the papers in class about two weeks later, he gave me a brief smile. Glancing at my paper, I quickly discovered why the assignment had been so difficult for me. I also understood my professor's smile. Although Ecclesiastes was the assignment's topic, I had based my responses on the apocryphal book Ecclesiasticus. Nevertheless, my professor still generously gave me a C−, albeit the lowest allowable passing grade. Right next to the grade, he commented, "Good effort, all things considered!"

—

Somehow, I managed to pass all my courses. The fantastic holiday tips arrived as expected, and I quit the paper route in early January. No more getting up so early each morning.

Things should have then started looking up for me, but that was not to be the case. An increasing skepticism about my call and suitability for ministry welled up within me. I turned increasingly to alcohol to keep my foreboding doubts at bay. Eventually, Helen began expressing serious concerns about my excessive drinking.

Alcohol-induced blackouts were pretty much a part of my drinking history dating back to the first semester at Queen's in 1967, when alcohol and I began our love affair. Since that time, no more than two weeks ever passed, aside from my alcohol/drug rehab experience in 1973, without me having a significant alcoholic blackout. When greeted by a blackout upon waking, I could sometimes gradually remember most of the previous evening's activities, yet on other occasions, huge chunks of time remained forever beyond my grasp.

—

Something happened on Monday morning, January 16, 1978, that really gave me pause for concern. I woke up alone in my room with a pounding headache. Everything was spinning. My heart felt like it was skipping a beat every few seconds, and saliva was nowhere to be found.

Daunting as this experience was, I had come to know this hellish terrain all too well, especially over the past five or six years. There was no reason to doubt that I couldn't once again slog through the muck and by early evening come out unscathed.

I eventually recalled meeting some friends to watch Sunday afternoon's Super Bowl football game between Dallas and Denver. Yet I couldn't remember anything about the game, the time spent with my friends, or returning to my room. My memory of those twelve hours was absolutely nil. Never before had my blackouts been so severe.

Having been a fan of the Dallas Cowboys and their coach, Tom Landry, for many years, I decided to go out and buy a newspaper from the nearby coin-operated paper box to find out who had won the game. Thankfully, I had slept in my clothes. Bending over to put on a pair of pants would have been disastrous. Puke was already queued up in my throat.

I soon found myself in front of the paper box and ready to buy my paper, but I was shaking so badly that any attempts at placing the change in the proper coin slots proved utterly futile. The coins kept missing their desired target and falling to the sidewalk. On the verge of returning to my room, I noticed a young boy about to walk by me. After saying that I was ill and needed his help, I was grateful that he put the coins in the box for me.

After tipping him, I immediately opened the paper and happily saw the score. Dallas had won the game; nevertheless, by the time I returned to my room, the game's outcome no longer mattered. I was shaking uncontrollably and could barely stand up. Lying down on my bed, I desperately clenched the covers to steady myself, still seeing coins falling to the sidewalk.

—

Later that same week, Helen decided to visit her father for the weekend. She wanted me to see her off at the bus terminal for the two-hour trip. I didn't want her to go but was unable to sway her decision. We decided to meet in one of the student pubs where I would be having a few cold ones with classmates after our Friday afternoon intramural hockey game.

When Helen arrived, I was drinking by myself, as all my teammates had left after having one or two beers. There had been a few times over the last decade when a surge of unbridled, mean-spirited energy suddenly engulfed me while I was drinking. Invariably on these binges, bedlam soon ruled. Today was one of those occasions.

I was well on my way to oblivion when Helen arrived. I not only didn't take Helen to the bus terminal, but I also publicly ridiculed and demeaned her. She left stunned, humiliated, and in tears. I ordered another beer.

—

No convenient blackout awaited me when I awoke the next morning. I was extremely hungover, yet my recall of the previous day's events, especially my behavior toward Helen, was crystal clear. As usual, I turned to my familiar morning-with-a-blackout routine.

Many times over the years when wallowing in shame and remorse after a previous night's aberrant antics, I fervently promised to quit drinking forever. But as I began to sober up and feel better, two things always happened. Invariably, quitting drinking quickly morphed into reducing drinking. Shortly afterward, even this watered-down version would be summarily dismissed.

This time, however, I didn't seek refuge in my usual alcohol self-assessment bullshit but rather began to see the situation with unexpected clarity. Initially, I focused on Helen. I wondered whether our relationship was still salvageable, or if the damage from her point of view was irreparable. Yet I soon realized that there was far more on the line than just our relationship. Drinking imperiled my last chance for a meaningful and fulfilling life.

My call to ministry had miraculously opened long-closed doors of hope and self-respect. In spite of my own strong and persisting self-doubts, others such as Dr. Morrison, the staff and Session of Timothy Eaton Memorial, my Sunday school lads, and Helen strongly believed in me; however, it was just a matter of time, probably sooner rather than later, when I'd be going off on some drunken, expletive-filled rant either in class or at the church. Surprisingly, part of me was really scared about where sobriety could possibly lead, but the thought of never having given this wondrous call to ministry my best shot was far scarier.

Feeling unmistakably prescient, I knew instinctively that the moment for the most important decision in my life had finally arrived. Sensing life or death hung in the balance, within a heartbeat I chose life. On January 21, 1978, I resolved to never have another drink of alcohol.

—

Later that day, I called Helen and apologized for my behavior. Begging her forgiveness, I promised to quit drinking. In accepting my contriteness, she also emphasized that our relationship would abruptly end should I ever break this promise. After our conversation, I made another key decision.

For years I smoked at least one pack of cigarettes a day, an amount that easily rose to two packs when drinking heavily. It struck me that my smoking and drinking might be triggers for each other. To ensure that smoking couldn't undermine my sobriety, I gave up cigarettes too. I also considered stopping smoking dope but just couldn't bring myself, at least for now, to part with my tried-and-true pacifier.

—

The first few weeks without any alcohol or cigarettes were much harder than I anticipated. Although the lure of a drink or a smoke often seemed impossible to resist, I somehow toed the line one day at a time. Distance running and lifting weights really helped to diffuse some of my anxiety. Helen's support proved invaluable.

Surprisingly, I found considerable solace in my rudimentary devotional life. Mom, who had finally come on board with my ordination aspirations, gave me her copy of Harry Emerson Fosdick's *The Meaning of Prayer*. The tone of Fosdick's prayers really spoke to me, as did his scriptural references and commentaries for each day of the week. Prayer was uncharted waters for me. Fosdick provided an essential framework that helped me begin to pray in my own way.

Certain Psalms from my Sunday school days also filled me with hope. Psalms 23 and 121 helped to steady me as I navigated this new and unsettling world of sobriety. Countless times each day, the Lord's Prayer served as my ballast and refuge.

Midway in the second semester, serendipity gifted me with Romans 8:38–39 while I just happened to be waiting for a class and thumbing through the Bible:

> "For I am sure that neither death nor life, nor angels nor rulers, nor things present nor things to come, nor powers, nor height nor depth, nor anything else in all creation, will be able to separate us from the love of God in Christ Jesus our Lord."

Although I never recalled having seen this passage of scripture before, the words felt as though they had been specifically earmarked for me right at that point in time.

—

Barring extenuating circumstances, United Church candidates for ordination were required to complete two different kinds of internships: a four-month summer mission field and a four-hundred-hour "unit" of Clinical Pastoral Education (CPE). Whereas the former usually took place in a rural setting assigned to candidates by the national church, the latter allowed candidates their choice of CPE training centers, usually in hospitals.

Daunting as it seemed, the mission field option appeared to offer the best opportunity for some firsthand experience of parish ministry, which I really needed at that point. Ordained ministers generally located within an hour's drive of each student's field placement provided weekly supervision and assistance. Like the rest of my class, I wouldn't be finding out my posting's location until early April.

—

Regardless of my internship's location, there was no getting around the fact that I would need a car. This posed a huge problem. Chalk up another way in which I was different from my classmates. This Sunday school teacher didn't even know how to drive! Growing up in a family without a car, I'd never learned to drive, unlike most of my high school classmates.

Having always lived in cities, I used public transportation. On those rare occasions when a car was needed, I ordered a cab. With my drinking history, not being able to drive had actually been a godsend. If I had known how to drive, there would have been countless occasions over the years for tragedy to strike. I could very well have killed myself, or even worse, killed other people.

Since Helen didn't have her license either, I checked out some driving school advertisements in the Yellow Pages phone directory. The programs were all very similar, so I just randomly picked one. I was assigned to a class with four much younger students and an instructor. During our six two-hour lessons, we learned the rules of the road while also taking turns behind the wheel with the instructor in the passenger seat. It was reassuring to see that the instructor had his own set of brakes just in case something bad was about to happen!

I felt quite tentative behind the wheel and was only able to parallel park successfully once in six attempts. Postponing the test for some additional practice time wasn't an option, as it was already late March. Within the next few days, my classmates and I would learn the details for our upcoming internships. Without a driver's license, my summer internship plans would grind to a halt, disrupting the entire ordination process itself.

I showed up for my test with only ninety minutes of actual driving experience from the group lessons. Having easily passed the written part of the assessment, it was now time to get behind the wheel next to the driving examiner. My hands were sweating so much that I almost lost my grip on the steering wheel. My mouth was parched. My vision was blurry. There was a high likelihood that I could become the first seminarian who couldn't begin a summer internship on account of not being able to drive a car.

An invisible herd of elephants was sitting on my chest. Security guard duty suddenly seemed like a more sensible career to pursue. I sure could have used a drink or a smoke but settled instead for a prayer. As the test progressed, I miraculously performed each task. Then came that dreaded command to "parallel park." I gave it my best shot but wasn't even close.

The examiner gave me one final chance. I silently offered a last desperate prayer. Time slowed down. The elephant herd moved off my chest.

I perfectly executed the maneuver. The examiner offered his congratulations and told me that I had successfully passed the test. Thankfully, another major hurdle was cleared.

—

Within a few days, I learned some details about my summer assignment. The "Smokey Burn/Battle Heights" mission field was located in northeastern Saskatchewan near the Manitoba border, just east of Carrot River. This city slicker would soon be going very rural.

Fortunately, I was able to contact my future supervisor, the Rev. Fred Seller. Fred was the minister of the Carrot River Pastoral Charge. He described the placement in general, and most importantly, provided me with the travel itinerary, which the United Church had already made on my behalf.

First up was a five-hour direct flight from Toronto to Saskatoon, one of the major cities in Saskatchewan. The next step involved a six-hour northerly bus trip to Nipawin, about ten miles from Carrot River, where Fred would meet me. Hearing that I didn't have a car, Fred said that he would keep an eye out for a good used vehicle for me. Even over the phone, I found Fred's kind manner very reassuring.

—

Like the first semester, I managed to pass all my courses. This second semester proved particularly challenging after I quit drinking and smoking in January. During those initial weeks of abstinence, a dense fog often enveloped me, turning my brain to mush.

Helen and I celebrated my overall B average for the entire year, knowing full well the transcript's limitations. It did not show grades for trusting my call to ministry, teaching Sunday school, delivering over three hundred morning newspapers for the entire first semester, quitting drinking and smoking, learning to drive, and getting my driver's license. With regards to this curriculum, my grades were solid "A's."

—

Before I left for the summer, Helen's father invited us for a weekend visit so that we could formally meet each other. When Helen and I worshiped with her father's congregation, he surprised us near the end of the service by introducing me as a young student minister heading west to serve the Lord.

After his enthusiastic endorsement, everyone prayed for me and wished me well. The timeliness of such an outpouring of support couldn't have come at a better time for me. My spirits lifted. I didn't feel so vulnerable and overwhelmed.

—

In preparing for the upcoming sixteen-week separation, Helen and I felt the need to formally stake our claim as a couple. We privately became engaged about a week before I headed west. Figuring that our future plans would work themselves out in due course, an actual wedding date at that point wasn't really necessary.

Although pretty well living with Helen ever since we'd met, I officially moved from my furnished room to her apartment. Our love had deepened over the past few months. We now felt strong enough to weather the upcoming pain from being apart. Promising to write regularly, we hoped periodic phone calls might be possible once I got the lay of the land.

Saskatchewan Summer Internship

In preparing for Saskatchewan, my most pressing fear was the flight itself. Although I was terrified of flying, there were no other feasible travel options. The trip by train or bus took far too long. In any event, the United Church had already purchased the plane tickets.

For my three previous flights as an adult, I'd always self-medicated with plenty of alcohol prior to boarding the plane. Yet even those stiff shots didn't prevent me from being afraid. Takeoffs and landings were downright nerve-wracking, as were those random, inexplicable noises from the plane's undercarriage.

Preparing to board, I was scared shitless. Even Helen commented on how pale I appeared. When presenting the boarding pass to the flight attendant, my hand trembled. Mercifully, the pilot announced prior to takeoff that the flight should be smooth with good weather the entire way.

During our recent visit, Helen's father had given me his treasured copy of Dr. John Baillie's *A Diary of Private Prayer* as a token of his support for me and my ministry. Like Fosdick's book, Baillie's also appealed to me. I was relying on these books, along with the Lord's Prayer, the twenty-third Psalm, and Romans 8:38–39 to keep my terror at bay over the next five hours.

Since there weren't many passengers on this flight, the seats on either side of me were vacant. No one saw how tightly I gripped the arm rests and squirmed in my seat during the flight's first two hours. I tried reading Fosdick and Baillie but was too anxious to comprehend the material. The Lord's Prayer and twenty-third Psalm quickly became my silent mantras, providing me with some semblance of refuge and strength.

Suddenly, halfway through the flight, my fears and anxieties inexplicably lifted. Daring to look out the window and survey God's grandeur in the magnificent cloud formations, I surprisingly felt calmer. Relaxing into my seat, I felt incredibly blessed, embarking on a remarkable summer adventure that would have been totally inconceivable eighteen months earlier.

To top things off, a flight attendant invited me to meet the captain in the cockpit if I wished. If she had asked me forty-five minutes earlier, I would have emphatically declined. The timing of this proposal could not have been better.

Upon returning to my seat after visiting with the pilot and co-pilot in the cockpit, I marveled at this incredulous turn of events. The most satisfying aspect of the entire experience was realizing that I hadn't needed a drink or a smoke to survive. The phrase "on a wing and a prayer" never seemed so apt.

After landing and stepping on terra firma, I intuitively knew something very important had occurred during the flight. Some embedded, destructive survival techniques no longer seemed so necessary. I sensed more wonders might await me.

—

The five-hour bus trip went as planned, with Fred waiting for me in Nipawin. Since it was fairly late, we only briefly touched base before hitting the hay in the manse. Over a hearty breakfast the following morning, I met Fred's wife and their young son. They were all quite friendly and helped me to feel as comfortable as possible.

My most pressing order of business involved the purchase of a 1970 Ford Fairlane, which Fred managed to reserve until I arrived. Given that I was the new student minister, the vehicle's asking price had been generously reduced. The car had low mileage and was in good condition; however, there was one humungous problem. The car had a standard transmission. My only driving experience—albeit ninety minutes in total—was behind the wheel of an automatic.

I had heard the terms "automatic transmission" and "standard transmission" but had no idea what they meant. Likewise, I was totally clueless about a "clutch." Even before getting behind the wheel, I knew that this new challenge could make parallel parking look like a walk in the park.

Thank heavens for Fred's incredible patience and expertise. He hung in there with me over the next several hours as I repeatedly ground the gears, stalling the car while attempting to drive back and forth in his long driveway. Finally, I got the hang of it and was good to go.

Fred helped me in many ways throughout the course of my summer internship, but his invaluable assistance and kind manner on "day one" was beyond measure.

—

Fred and I spent the rest of my first day going over some details about the mission field itself. I checked out some previous worship bulletins, which provided the general worship format with which my new parishioners would be familiar. Yet seeing that at least three hymns were typically sung each Sunday, I immediately felt skittish.

As someone who couldn't carry a tune even if my life depended on it, I always felt self-conscious whenever singing. I hesitatingly shared my anxiety about the substantial hymn-singing portion of the services with Fred. He good-naturedly told me, "Make a joyful noise unto the Lord" and let the rest take care of itself.

Fred told me that although my new digs didn't have any running water, there was a well with a hand-pump near one side of the cabin. An outhouse was also close by on the other side. I was relieved to learn that the cabin itself had electricity. A refrigerator, toaster, and small heating element were presumably all in good working order.

Given that there was no running water, I was particularly interested in the shower arrangements. For the past several years, a family down the road a few miles from the cabin made their own shower available to student ministers. Interestingly, Fred said that although the students greatly appreciated the showers, the piece of homemade pie set aside for them on the kitchen counter was in fact what the interns relished most.

Since there wasn't a phone in the cabin, this same family also made their personal phone available, as long as student ministers covered the cost of any calls. Over the course of the summer, Helen and I arranged a time once a month when she would call me. Our ninety-minute conversations, as well as our weekly letters, served as "relationship life-lines" during this interminable period of separation.

—

Heading out the next day for Smokey Burn and Battle Heights, we first stopped at Carrot River's main grocery store so that I could stock up on provisions for the upcoming week. Fred encouraged me to do my grocery shopping in town after my weekly supervisory sessions with him. Since there wouldn't be any nearby convenience stores to purchase any forgotten items, I was advised to make a shopping list beforehand.

After shopping, we drove out caravan-style for about fourteen miles until stopping at the former one-room schoolhouse in Battle Heights. Except for occasional community events, this building's sole use over the past several years had been for summer worship services and the traditional week-long vacation Bible school. In spite of considerable longevity, my first church with its reddish-color and white trim was in remarkably good shape.

After driving the next ten miles to Smokey Burn, I finally beheld my new digs: a small, one-room cabin about one hundred yards from a larger, long abandoned, one-room schoolhouse. Both structures stood alone in a large field without anything else in sight. Even from a distance, it was obvious that they had long since seen their best days.

Entering the cabin, I immediately saw the abundance of "TLC" that had gone into making my new home as pleasant and clean as possible. The bed, table, chairs, desk, and lamps were all strategically situated, giving the cabin a very homey feel. There was a good-sized sink—which drained outside—as well as two large plastic containers for washing my hands and dishes.

However, it wasn't until the next day that I noticed the cabin's most important feature. Its screens were in excellent shape, and any cracks in the cabin itself had been tightly caulked. In other words, my new home was completely mosquito proofed.

I quickly learned that mosquitoes in this part of the country were huge, ravenous, and plentiful. Over the course of the summer, returning at night after visiting parishioners always proved hazardous. Try as I might, it was impossible to run the short distance from my car to the cabin without getting bitten several times. Night forays to the outhouse were made only when absolutely necessary.

After I got the lay of the land, Fred and I drove over to meet some of my new parishioners. Without exception, the warmth and care extended to me that day and for the entire summer was beyond anything that I could have imagined. They welcomed me into their lives at a time when I was most vulnerable.

—

Driving to my first worship service at Battle Heights a few days later, I couldn't help but marvel at what was transpiring. I felt immense gratitude for such an unfolding awesome adventure. Arriving at the church, I was greeted with welcoming smiles, open arms, and friendly handshakes.

My fear about the hymn singing was quickly laid to rest by the vibrant voices of the forty to fifty congregants of all ages. A few excellent singers and a very capable pianist sealed the deal! There were substantially more women than men in attendance. Given this area's short growing season, most men at this time were hard at work in the fields.

To my great surprise, hymn singing over the course of the summer actually touched me more than anything else in the worship service. Hymns such as "I Love to Tell the Story," "Softly and Tenderly Jesus Is Calling," "I am Thine, O Lord," and "Tell Me the Old, Old Story" always uplifted my spirits and soothed me.

But nothing ever topped "Amazing Grace." Whenever we sang this hymn by John Newton, feelings of joy and thankfulness, especially during the first verse, would so overwhelm me that I actually had to stop singing for a few moments to regain my composure.

> Amazing grace! How sweet the sound,
> That saved a wretch like me!
> I once was lost, but now am found;
> Was blind, but now I see.

Aside from worship and pastoral care, my additional responsibilities also proved enriching. I served for a week as a counselor at a United Church Presbytery Camp about two hundred miles away, directed a local week-long vacation Bible school for about forty children, and also led the church's youth group, which had energy to burn.

—

The heating element and toaster served me well throughout the summer and enabled me to make my own breakfasts and light lunches. After breakfast, I normally spent about two hours attending to my daily devotional work. Passages from Fosdick, Baillie, and a biblical lectionary nicely supplemented my regular Bible readings. This practice of setting some time aside each morning for spiritual reflection and prayer proved invaluable that summer and also set a devotional precedent for years to come.

By using a lectionary for my sermon preparation over the course of the summer, I became much more familiar with the Bible. For each Sunday's worship, the lectionary provided an Old Testament reading, a

Psalm, a Gospel reading and an additional New Testament selection. At times, I almost deviated from the lectionary when none of the selections struck me as relevant. However, I stayed with the process, and invariably some direction for the sermon revealed itself.

The lectionary also helped reinforce my budding sense of personal discipline. During the course of each week, the lectionary's Bible passages became my companions, stimulating and nurturing me in ways I hadn't anticipated. By the time Sunday worship came around, these readings felt like good companions who accompanied me throughout the worship service, especially when I was preaching.

Following my daily devotions, I usually had a good six to ten mile run along the shoulder of the highway. Upon hearing that I was a distance runner, one of my elderly parishioners had enthusiastically remarked, "Out here, son, you can run to your heart's content!" Following a good run, I headed out for my shower, where fresh towels and homemade pie awaited.

—

After I had been on the job for about three weeks, a specific event set the tone for my overall summer experience. I was invited to the annual round-up in which most of the area's cattle were herded a few miles down the main road to better seasonal pastures. This was always a very exciting occasion, especially for the children, when people of all ages proudly sported their western finery.

I just planned on being a spectator, but my congregants had a surprise in store for me. Kindly taking my city roots into account, they gave me a small pony called Lucky to ride rather than one of the large horses ridden by the real cowpokes. Since my parishioners were primed to assess the mettle of their new summer pastor, I didn't see any viable way of ducking this well-intentioned rite of passage!

Lucky's diminutive stature and unassuming nature soon put my misgivings to rest. While sitting bareback on Lucky and gripping the reins, I joined everyone else amid great fanfare. However, lest I became too enamored with my new "home on the range" persona, Lucky eventually tested this cowpoke wannabe by suddenly bolting at full speed with me frantically holding on to her neck for dear life.

In the face of calamity, I visualized a story in the local newspaper: "Ride on children's pony reveals new student minister from Toronto is no Buffalo Bill!" But just when all hope seemed lost, Lucky miraculously slowed down, thereby saving my dignity and quite possibly my life. Several folks gave me kudos for not falling off yet also good-naturedly encouraged me to keep my "day" job.

—

During my first weeks, "clouds" suddenly caught my attention. It was as though I was seeing them for the very first time in my life. With the skyline uninterrupted except for the crops in the fields, clouds could fully display their scope and formations. The sight of a storm coming from far off in the distance was a sight that continually blew me away.

Later in the summer, mile after mile of yellow rape and purple flax coming into bloom dazzled and humbled me. Whenever I beheld this swaying magnificence, the hair on the back of my neck never failed to rise.

———

With so many intangibles, such as weather conditions and machinery breakdowns, my parishioners were never sure what the next day might entail; therefore, scheduled pastoral visits weren't practical for them. Although just showing up unannounced at parishioners' homes was initially awkward for me, this manner of pastoral visitation soon felt like second nature.

I normally made one visit per day, spending several hours assisting my congregation members in the fields or helping them with their large gardens. Afterward, we all enjoyed a hardy supper consisting of their own beef, pork, and chicken as well as vegetables right from their gardens. No meal was ever complete without homemade dessert and a good cup of coffee.

My willingness to assist with strenuous outdoor chores, to converse without any preachy overtones, and to enjoy some good give-and-take earthy banter really helped me bond with the men right from the get-go. The fact that I didn't smoke or drink seemed particularly appealing to the women. Being engaged was also seen in a favorable light. Surprisingly, most folks also liked the fact that I seemed "rough around the edges."

—

Although many of my parishioners had quit school early to help their families make ends meet, this lack of formal education didn't detract from their wisdom and good old-fashioned common sense. I felt privileged listening to them tell their stories, and they seemed at ease candidly sharing with me. After the kids had gone to bed, our conversations around a kitchen table well-stocked with toothpicks were a beautiful blend of small talk and serious discourse, touching me deeply.

My internship wasn't without formidable personal challenges. Just like those summers in Sudbury as a teenager, I was the new dude in town, and the local talent at Carrot River's Saturday night dances was there for the taking. No longer paralyzed by teenage inhibitions, I now commanded a full repertoire of proven "night moves." Though shaky at times, my fidelity to Helen remained intact throughout the summer.

—

Helen flew out to join me for my last worship service. After receiving a splendid send-off, Helen and I drove out through the Canadian Rockies to Vancouver. Although the scenery was truly magnificent, we seemed out of synch with each other.

We found ourselves constantly disagreeing over a myriad of small logistical details, such as where to eat, where to stay, and what to do. Although this new dynamic proved troubling, we figured it was just part of getting used to each other again after our four-month separation. Thankfully, we never went to sleep harboring any grudges.

The trip's highlight for me was visiting Dr. Morrison and his wife in their Vancouver retirement digs. After I sold my car for a small loss, Helen joined me in flying back to Toronto on standby.

—

My Saskatchewan summer mission field experience was nothing short of transformational on several fronts. Returning to Toronto, I had a much better understanding of parish ministry along with newfound confidence about becoming a minister. Moreover, I was recovering my moral compass and savoring a budding sense of self-respect.

Emmanuel College: Second Year

Before returning to Emmanuel, I received word that my congregational responsibilities at Timothy Eaton Memorial had changed. Closing the chapter on my short Sunday school stint, I now became a co-leader of the church's youth group. I was going to miss my lads and hoped this new tour of duty would prove as satisfying.

Over the next seven months, the group met bi-weekly, with an overnight outing as the grand finale. There were about twenty youth group members, ranging in age from thirteen to sixteen, with slightly more girls than boys. The other co-leader was a few years younger than me. Like me, she was also a neophyte with this kind of gig. We got along well and worked effectively together.

All in all, the youth group proved to be fun and meaningful for everyone. The co-leaders even survived those occasional attempted coupes against authority for which teenagers are most renowned.

—

After such an enriching internship in Saskatchewan, I feared that my second year at Emmanuel would just be another survival boot camp for me, like first year. But within the first month, I realized something new was afoot. Time seemed to slow down, giving me a window of sorts to process information quicker and with greater clarity.

Throughout my first year, I often felt like an interloper who somehow finagled his way into seminary life. Feeling more legitimate now as a seminarian, I began participating more in classes, picking my spots to discuss assignments with peers and professors alike. Budding first-year friendships, mostly with fellow Emmanuel "jocks," took on greater depth and enjoyment for me.

—

In the first semester, I took a course called "The Theology of Jesus Christ," offered at St. Michael's College. St. Michael's, like Emmanuel, was one of seven denominational seminaries (two other Catholic colleges, two Anglican colleges, and one Presbyterian college) that comprised the Toronto School of Theology. This course at Saint Michael's College helped me to reflect about the historical Jesus, how he might have understood himself, and what kinds of feelings and experiences he might have had. The course's professor encouraged me to use the major essay assignment to explore and articulate my own evolving Christology.

Seizing this creative opportunity, I used my paper's thesis to challenge traditional theology concerning the historical Jesus' ability to completely understand and appreciate the full scope of the human condition if he, unlike everyone else, had never sinned. In grading my paper, the professor very adeptly critiqued it and encouraged me to sharpen my very rudimentary skills in critical thinking. Nevertheless, she still gave me my first A at seminary for having presented a systematic theological inquiry in a candid, comprehensive, and genuine manner. I couldn't have asked for a better shot in the arm.

—

Midway through the first semester, I was asked to meet with a small committee from the United Church's Toronto Conference. This committee traditionally met with all the conference ordinands to assess each candidate's potential for ministry and to offer assistance as needed. I heard via the grapevine that sometimes in previous years the committee had been known to ask single ordinands about their commitment to celibacy until married.

Helen and I discussed various ways for me to respond if this line of questioning arose in the meeting. We ardently agreed that if asked, I would be completely honest about our relationship, cohabitation, and engagement, even if such disclosures permanently derailed my ordination plans. Thankfully, the interview went very smoothly without any specific inquiries about my personal life.

—

Shortly afterward I faced a much more formidable challenge. Like the rest of my second-year classmates who aspired to be United Church ministers, I was required to complete a comprehensive set of psychological tests. These mandatory tests were designed to identify possible dynamics, traits, and attitudes that could seriously affect one's overall potential and suitability for ministry.

Joining my classmates, I began the three-hour evaluation process, albeit with a high degree of wariness. Although my recent summer internship really helped to validate my calling, deep down I still doubted having the right stuff for ministry. These tests could very well confirm such doubts were quite justified.

The test was made up of several varied components that covered such topics as one's ancestral history, childhood, teen and adult years, as well as relationships with family, friends, peers, and authority figures. There were multiple choice and fill-in-the blank questions as well as a section for a brief biographical narrative. In addition, there was a component for a self-sketch in whatever manner or context one chose.

The psychologist administering the test instructed us to be as spontaneous as possible with our responses rather than overthinking them. There were times in the test when I thought that some of the questions were exactly the same or just slightly different than previous ones already answered. Although tempted to look back at my previous responses, I abided by the psychologist's opening instructions.

In spite of my misgivings about the testing, I answered the questions as honestly as possible. I knew that my ordinand status could soon be heading south regardless of whatever response-strategy was adopted. At least by being forthright, I could exit stage left with my sprouting integrity intact.

—

About a month later, the psychologist met with each of us individually to discuss the test results before submitting his report to the United Church's personnel department. I wouldn't have been surprised in the least if mine labeled me as unsuitable for ministry. Prior to the interview, I even told Helen that her father would most likely remain the only ordained "Gordon" in the family.

As things turned out, I didn't have to start pursuing security guard openings. The psychologist had indeed found some areas of significant concern that could adversely affect my future ministry if unaddressed. Yet he still affirmed my vocational path.

My self-sketch was of particular interest to the psychologist. I had sketched myself as a solitary football player running down the field and trying to catch a football that was just beyond my outstretched hands. I was clad in full football body armor. Since I was wearing a helmet, my face was completely hidden. Even without psychological training, I got the gist of what this sketch revealed about me.

The psychologist remarked how these test results consistently showed my deep ambivalence toward myself, my parents, and life in general, and also indicated some strong underlying feelings such as rage, shame, and fear. Rather than upsetting me, these findings were actually very helpful because they validated some painful truths I had sensed for years.

During a second meeting, which I requested, we discussed the test results in more depth as well as some options for follow up support. The psychologist thought that the university's counseling department could provide the kind of therapeutic assistance he felt I needed. When our meeting ended, the psychologist affirmed my initiative in requesting an additional session with him and for having been open to his recommendations regarding future therapeutic support.

—

Within a few days, I contacted the University of Toronto's student counseling services and scheduled an intake assessment with one of the psychiatrists on staff. In spite of considerable apprehension about entering the therapeutic arena, I knew this kind of professional support was essential for me. Although coping much better, I still felt an increasing, inexplicable uneasiness that everything could blow up at the drop of a hat.

My self-sketch as a fully-padded football player underscored why I needed therapy in the first place. I was weary from wearing all of that "armor" acquired over the years. I wanted to feel less guarded and more engaged. I felt a growing resolve to radically change my life's defining narrative, regardless of the challenges ahead.

—

Though not initially feeling much of a connection with my psychiatrist, Dr. Smith (name has been changed), I quickly sensed that he really knew his craft. This quality appealed to me and helped me feel at ease.

I told him about the psychologist's feedback, especially about my self-sketch. With Dr. Smith's prompting over the next several sessions, I candidly shared about my life ever since childhood. Although I wasn't sure where all of this was going, I believed he could help me eventually get to a point where some armor could be shed.

The importance of my alcoholic sobriety at that time could never really be overstated, yet I realized very early in therapy that emotional sobriety was necessary as well. Without identifying and addressing my core areas of dysfunction, I would stay stuck as a dry drunk, as someone who never grew up.

My first semester's grades showed significant improvement. I even received three As. Helen and I toasted this occasion with glasses of ginger ale.

—

Early in my second semester, Helen and I enrolled in an eight-week pre-marriage course at Timothy Eaton, even though we weren't planning to marry for at least another year. Hoping to complete her Master of Arts degree in the spring, Helen planned to earn some income by teaching part-time while also trying her hand at creative writing. If everything went well on my end, I'd be ordained sometime in May 1980.

In spite of our still somewhat nebulous wedding plans, Helen and I felt that this course might offer some immediate benefits. Over the last few months, we rarely went more than a few days without some kind of heated disagreement. Although this argumentative dynamic initially surfaced during the recent trip through the Canadian Rockies, our current ability to resolve any fallout had become much more protracted and guarded.

The two course facilitators, Pat and Ron MacKay, were a married couple themselves. The fact that I had already met Pat, who was on the staff at Timothy Eaton Memorial, felt reassuring to me. Ten other couples took the course as well. Pat and Ron helped everyone explore different relational topics, such as communication, fighting fair, and conflict resolution. The role plays were very effective and often a lot of fun.

Although Helen and I found the weekly classes worthwhile, our forty-five-minute walk home after each class proved much more informative. Without fail, as soon as Helen and I left the church, we began arguing about each other's behaviors and responses during the preceding session. These condemnatory discourses ramped up so quickly that often by the time we returned home, the original source of our mutual discord had been completely forgotten.

—

After completing the course, I began having serious reservations about our relationship, let alone any marriage plans. I still loved Helen, but I couldn't deny what the recent pre-marriage course experience so clearly revealed.

My major misgivings about our relationship and future together initially perplexed me. Helen and I were each seeing different therapists who helped us with our respective areas of dysfunction. Since each of us was realizing considerable personal growth, we naturally figured our relationship would benefit as well; however, with Dr. Smith's assistance, I painfully saw that our respective therapeutic gains had ironically changed the dynamic of our relationship to the point where we were no longer compatible and happy together. In fact, we were now much different individuals than those who fell in love only eighteen months earlier. Though helpful, these insights brought me face-to-face with a heart-wrenching dilemma.

I knew in my bones that our relationship needed to end, yet I also still loved Helen and knew that our love for each other had been the real deal. Given those feelings, I didn't know what to do.

Nonetheless, I eventually came to the realization that my love for Helen and my need to end our relationship were not mutually exclusive. By ending the relationship, I wasn't tainting or minimizing the love we genuinely felt for each other. Thankfully, our parting, though mutually upsetting, was as respectful as possible.

—

With Dr. Smith's help, I started to see how fear had been insidiously controlling many aspects of my life. This new awareness proved difficult and humbling for me. For a few days, I seriously considered quitting therapy. However, upon recalling my self-sketch and the weight of the armor, I returned for the next session.

I began to recognize how buffers such as alcohol, drugs, and other forms of reckless behavior had shielded me from my fears. Finely-honed defenses of disdain, arrogance, bravado, and sexual promiscuity protected me by keeping people at a distance. But at the end of the day, with the exception of sports and games, I was always left very lonely and isolated.

I was sorry when my sessions with Dr. Smith ended for the summer. In the fall, I wanted to better understand my fears and address them more fully. I also felt a need to explore my family's psychodynamics. Dr. Smith affirmed my therapeutic gains thus far, and he encouraged me to have a good summer before we resumed our work in the fall.

—

After receiving official word about my second year's B+ average, I immediately headed over to Timothy Eaton Memorial and shared this great news with the staff. This semester had been particularly satisfying for me in terms of my creative thinking, academic inquiry, and self-expression. I also had another highlight to share with them as well.

Just before classes ended, I surprised my professors and colleagues, none more than myself, by winning the Mrs. F.N.G. Starr Prize for Reading Scripture. This prize included a $100 honorarium. Although this cash would certainly come in handy, winning the prize itself against some pretty stiff peer competition filled me with boundless delight.

—

While chatting with Charlie Plaskett at the church, I shared about the recent break-up with Helen and my urgent need for a furnished room and a part-time job to cover living expenses. Always willing to lend an ear to those in need, Charlie listened patiently to my tale of woes. Once I finished talking, he said that he might have a solution to my problems but first needed to make some calls.

Meeting again with Charlie the next day as he suggested, I learned the results of his inquiries. I was dumbfounded by what he told me. His proposed solution involved the Ina Grafton Gage Home, a very sizable United Church residential facility for elderly women. Apparently, there was a decent-paying job opening for a part-time receptionist from 4:30–8:30 p.m. on weekdays. If interested in the job, I could also live there rent-free in the attic. Sensing my bewilderment, Charlie drove me over to the facility so that I could check things out for myself.

If there was ever an offer that couldn't be refused, this was it. A handshake sealed the deal in less than five minutes. My new accommodation package included a good-sized furnished bedroom, a full private bathroom, and a small sitting room. Not only would my linens and towels be changed each week, but the entire living quarters would be regularly cleaned as well.

Talk about manna from heaven. I would be the attic's sole occupant, as everyone else either lived or worked on the floors below me. I affectionately christened my new digs the "Home" and loved its location close to the subway and downtown. I thanked Charlie profusely.

I moved in immediately. With a month to spare before starting the next summer internship, this novice receptionist, after some initial training, jumped into the breach. Although the job itself primarily involved answering the phone, I also sold stamps and other small confectionary items to residents who, more often than not, invariably just dropped by for a good visit. I thoroughly enjoyed these ladies, and they seemed to enjoy me too.

My situation at the Home also proved extremely advantageous in another most unanticipated way. Whenever I met women at a nightclub or house party, sooner or later our conversations usually came around to what we did and where we lived. Most were amazed that I was not only studying for the ministry but also living and working in a home for elderly ladies. Although some of them immediately wrote me off as wacked, others just couldn't resist checking things out for themselves via the Home's fire escape stairs. I was more than happy to oblige!

Clinical Pastoral Education: Whitby Psychiatric Hospital

Having successfully completed my mission field placement the prior summer in Saskatchewan, I now needed to meet the four-hundred-hour "unit" of Clinical Pastoral Education (CPE) internship requirement for ordination. CPE programs were offered primarily in hospitals and occasionally in other institutional settings, such as prisons. Usually ordinands opted for intensive units (five days/week over ten consecutive weeks), although some chose the extended units (two days/week over several months).

I knew very little about CPE and having no desire to become a hospital chaplain, this mandatory requirement felt senseless. But in mid-January I applied to all three of the general hospital intensive programs in downtown Toronto, as these were the only training centers close to public transportation. In spite of not having a car, I also applied to an intensive program about thirty miles east of Toronto in Whitby, but I never seriously considered this option as viable given its location.

—

My hopes were riding on at least one of the Toronto programs coming through for me; however, my applications were rejected outright as these programs were already filled. Needing a miracle, my hopes immediately shifted to the Whitby Psychiatric Hospital program. Thankfully, I was offered an interview with that program's supervisor, the Rev. Dr. Grant Schwartz, which proved fortuitous in many ways.

First and foremost, I was accepted. Furthermore, Grant helped me to see how CPE could both enhance my pastoral skills and deepen my self-understanding. I didn't need any convincing to know that both these areas for me needed considerable development. As an added bonus, the Home's executive director, when informed of the CPE program's location, graciously suspended my receptionist responsibilities during this internship period.

Since the program began in early May, my friend Dave Smith drove me to Whitby in late April so that I could secure a furnished room. Unfortunately, my best housing option was six miles away from the hospital. Undeterred, I braced myself for plenty of walking and hoped for a dry summer.

As luck would have it, one of my classmates lived in Whitby and would be also taking this same program. After hearing about my situation, he kindly offered to give me a lift to and from the hospital each day.

To make things even better, the frequent bus service between Whitby and Toronto made spending weekends in the big city very doable when not on-call at the hospital. To top things off, Timothy Eaton Memorial provided the icing on the cake by surprising me with a very generous, unsolicited stipend to cover my summer expenses.

—

In each CPE program, students were responsible for providing pastoral care as part of a collaborative team of other healthcare professionals (i.e., physicians, nurses, social workers) in certain locations within the facility. Students would subsequently reflect on their respective pastoral experiences and then share such introspection with each other and the supervisor. We soon learned that this process was much easier said than done.

Part of a student's weekly homework invariably involved writing the dreaded "verbatim." This arduous, comprehensive process involved some variation of the following components: a word-for-word description, like a play, of a specific pastoral visit as well as a thorough analysis of one's feelings and motives as the visit itself unfolded; a critique of one's pastoral responses and clinical interventions; a statement about any insights gained from the experience; and a summary of the visit with some form of theological reflection.

Every day when we all met as a group, a student sat on the proverbial "hot seat" and presented their verbatim, followed by questions and feedback from their peers and supervisor. To each student's chagrin, a verbatim always provided great grist for the mill regardless of its content. Depending on each CPE supervisor's preference, there were always a number of other written exercises and challenging role-plays for stimulating a student's reflective process.

The actual timing of my respective mandatory summer internships proved critical for me. Without the benefit of my Saskatchewan experience and the subsequent therapeutic support from Dr. Smith, I would have found the CPE process far too threatening and surely would have bailed within the first few weeks.

—

As ordination candidates, my peers and I were all required to take a unit of CPE. Aside from my classmate, there were two women and two other men, as well as Grant, in my placement. Age-wise I was probably near the middle, with everyone being within fifteen years of each other. Two students were from different denominational seminaries, and another student was a year behind me at Emmanuel.

Within the first week, I realized how this arduous CPE experience perfectly dovetailed with my therapeutic gains with Dr. Smith. Once this insight hit home, I quickly embraced the CPE process. On the other hand, some of my peers initially found the inherent rigors of this introspective process very difficult, and resisted identifying or discussing their own problematic issues.

Among many other things, my first unit of CPE taught me that even decent, responsible individuals like my peers and supervisor, had their own areas of personal dysfunction. I wasn't the only one with issues.

—

Each of us was required to lead a worship service at the hospital on two separate Sundays during the program. These services were attended by many patients as well as several staff members responsible for the patients' care. Since some of the patients' family members also attended, the average size of a Sunday congregation was about eighty. On those weekends when it was my turn to lead the Sunday services, I stayed in Whitby and relied on taxis for transportation.

In the first week, Grant gave us a heads-up about what might arise during these services. We learned that some patient's screaming or sobbing, constant rocking, or spontaneous standing and sitting was bound at some point to take us by surprise. He gently challenged us to find our own ways to pastorally intervene without relinquishing our role as the worship service's leader.

—

My initial Sunday assignment came early in the program and filled me with considerable anxiety. Thankfully, my nerves settled down once the service started, allowing me to feel genuinely connected to congregants.

All in all, everything seemed to be going along smoothly. I felt a growing sense of competence and confidence, anticipating nothing other than clear sailing as we all began singing the concluding hymn, "Stand Up, Stand Up for Jesus."

Then during the second verse, a stocky, middle-aged man suddenly stood up and walked into the center aisle. He seemed to adopt a kind of military "at attention" pose, with his arms straight down at his sides. Shortly afterward, he began approaching me, swinging his arms as if formally marching. As he got closer, I saw some of the hospital staff also moving forward, but it was quite obvious that this patient would reach me first.

I was aware of a few options, like distancing myself from the patient or putting up my fists in self-defense. However, I didn't flinch and kept on singing. When he was about a foot away from me, the patient stopped abruptly, quickly raised his right arm, saluted me, dropped his arm, turned around, and marched back to his seat. Afterward, some staff members affirmed my response to this incident, thereby giving me a good boost of confidence. Not having flinched was particularly satisfying for me.

—

Nothing in the program challenged me more than my peer relationships. As with most initial CPE units, the typical three-week honeymoon period of just being nice to each other invariably breaks down when one or two students start interjecting criticism, constructive or otherwise, into their peer feedback. Such input radically changes the group dynamic, and relationships can quickly fray.

Various peer alliances, often very labile in nature, are formed and re-formed over the course of the program. Our group was no different. Although my peers and I initially bonded with an unspoken yet mutually assumed "I've got your back and you've got mine" sense of solidarity, such a stance didn't last long.

Conflict resolution was unquestionably my most challenging lesson in this unit of CPE. Throughout my life whenever experiencing conflict, I indubitably responded with well-targeted, lethal sarcasm. Although conflict always invigorated me, I usually found that others did not feel similarly.

Sometime around the program's fourth week, it became apparent that two of my peers and I really didn't like each other. After a few days of implied contempt, we heatedly aired our substantial animosities toward each other during an afternoon group session. Whereas my peers weren't used to expressing feelings such as rage and disdain, I came out with guns a-blazing, taking no prisoners. In my next weekly supervisory session, Grant helped me thoroughly examine this peer altercation, as well as conflict in general.

The CPE's process itself gave me a kind of laboratory for trying out new conflict resolution strategies that conveyed a sense of civility, respect, and goodwill. Although very difficult at first, I tried my best to restore these fractured peer relationships. Surprisingly, I felt unexpectedly uplifted just by making the reconciliatory effort itself. I was grateful that my efforts in this regard were also reciprocated in varying degrees by my peers.

In our own way, my peers and I experienced considerable soul-searching with many intense, emotional highs and lows over the course of the program. We found great joy and meaning in recovering our collective goodwill and genuinely empathizing with each other's vulnerabilities and personal struggles. We also benefitted from our supervisor, who helped us maintain a fairly healthy balance between affirmation and constructive criticism within CPE's unique introspective and intrapersonal learning crucible.

—

During my CPE experience, I ministered to acute psychiatric patients, psycho-geriatric patients, and their families. I learned much about human suffering, debilitating mental illness, human heartbreak and resilience, devoted selfless care, and unshakable hope. Collaborating with other healthcare professionals and feeling valued as part of their team was something I relished and enjoyed. To my surprise, hospital chaplaincy now seemed very meaningful and fulfilling.

After completing the program, I felt enriched beyond measure. Returning for my third and final year at Emmanuel, I noticed both a bounce and a purpose in my step. At almost twenty-nine years of age, I was finally starting to grow up.

Emmanuel College: Third Year

Upon returning to Emmanuel for my third year, I immediately resumed my weekly therapy sessions with Dr. Smith. Those previous meetings with him during my second year had been very helpful in their own right and had also served as a catalyst for continuing my inner work during the summer's unit of CPE. Not to disparage my therapeutic gains thus far, I knew it was now time for some heavy lifting.

Beginning this final year at seminary, my self-confidence still waned considerably when I compared myself to my classmates, especially in terms of suitability for ministry. As someone about to be ordained in less than a year, I felt alarmingly deficient both personally and professionally. Meaningful course selections and field education experiences were critically important for me at this juncture.

—

During last year's second semester, I took the course "Psychological Aspects of Prayer & Spiritual Life" at Regis College, another Catholic seminary within the ecumenical Toronto School of Theology. When taking the course, I'd been too caught up in those last months of my relationship with Helen to really delve into the fascinating material. Nonetheless, I had still enjoyed the course's professor and even whetted my spiritual hunger with some brief exposure to the ascetic traditions of the Desert Fathers and Mothers, as well as to the Spiritual Exercises of St. Ignatius of Loyola.

I yearned for more depth in my spiritual life. To help meet this need, I returned to Regis College and enrolled in the course "Psychotherapy & Spiritual Direction." The fact that this course was being taught by that same professor was an added bonus. Entering Regis College once again, I sensed good things were in store for me. After the summer's enriching

CPE experience, I felt more grounded. This time around, I was wide open to whatever awaited me.

Although many aspects of the course proved relevant, the process of spiritual direction was by far the most meaningful. Assigned by the college to a spiritual director on campus, I learned some of the basics of a particular form of disciplined spiritual practice in which I would sit quietly for twenty minutes each morning and evening with selected passages of scripture, noting any words or phrases that seemed evocative. Immediately after each sit, I wrote down my reflections about the overall experience as candidly as possible in a journal.

Some of the scriptural passages for reflection involved various biblical stories about Jesus, which I fondly recalled from childhood. In particular, the "prodigal son" (Luke 15:11–32), the "good Samaritan" (Luke 10:29–37), the "lost sheep" (Luke 15:3–7), and the raising of Lazarus (John 11:38–44) were among my favorites. Stories such as these involved themes of mercy, forgiveness, restoration, healing, and wholeness, which touched me deeply.

My spiritual director, with whom I met weekly during that fall semester, didn't talk very much but rather served as a kind of non-judgmental, affirming spiritual witness. He helped me discern what my journal reflections were possibly revealing and encouraged me to stay with the process, especially when the practice itself frequently seemed too demanding. At a time when I was striving for greater spiritual depth and increased personal transparency, this particular course couldn't have been more opportune.

—

In addition to the two mandatory summer internships, all United Church of Canada ordinands were also required to complete a field placement, which typically began in late September and ended in mid-April. Since this kind of internship invariably took place in a parish setting, the pastors of those participating congregations supervised their own respective students. Like my classmates, I knew the field placements usually involved a weekly commitment of at least two partial days/evenings during the week as well as worship services on Sunday mornings.

Without having a clue as to which field placement might best meet my myriad of needs, I anxiously perused the newly-posted list of openings, desperately hoping that the right fit for me would miraculously reveal itself. Not having a car and needing to rely solely on public transportation, I quickly eliminated many of the postings based on the commuting times required.

Of the remaining realistic placement options, Saint Luke's United Church in downtown Toronto caught my attention. This inner-city location at the intersection of Sherbourne Street and Carlton Street wasn't completely unknown to me, as I had occasionally passed through there late at night on my way to bars in other neighborhoods.

On those midnight prowls, I invariably saw an array of alcoholics, drug addicts, pimps, prostitutes, and other homeless people out on the streets. Not once on these jaunts did I ever reflect about the possible predicating factors that had landed these individuals in such dire straits. Nor had it ever occurred to me during those times that I could very well have been joining them.

There was no denying the fact that an internship at Saint Luke's was bound to offer something markedly different from my predominantly white, upper-middle to upper class congregational frame of reference. A Saint Luke's internship would surely hurl me from my narrow comfort zone. My soul surprisingly stirred.

Without even checking out any of the other possible placements, I immediately met with Emmanuel's field education director and expressed my interest in Saint Luke's. He told me that many former students had benefitted greatly from this placement, especially from the Rev. Malcolm Finlay's supervision. Later that same day, I called the Rev. Finlay and arranged to meet him the following morning at the church.

Sitting down with Malcolm in his office, I couldn't help noticing his friendly and hospitable demeanor. He took quite an interest in my call to ministry and my experience thus far with the ordination process. Of particular interest to him were my reasons for considering Saint Luke's as a field placement. After listening to me, Malcolm talked about his own background as well as some of the history of Saint Luke's.

Next, he showed me the sanctuary, which was much larger than I anticipated, as well as the much smaller and more intimate adjacent chapel. The church's beautifully detailed woodwork and the lovely stained-glass windows seemed warm and inviting. Upon returning to his office, Malcolm offered me the Saint Luke's field placement. In less than a heartbeat, I accepted his offer. As I was leaving, Malcolm introduced me to the church's secretary and custodian, who both extended a very warm welcome.

A few days later, I joined Malcolm for Sunday worship, during which time he officially introduced me to his congregation as their new student minister. While standing next to him, I felt well received by the two hundred or so congregants. Several parishioners personally greeted me in the coffee hour and fellowship time following the service. After leaving the church and riding the subway back to the Home, I had a gut feeling that a marvelous learning opportunity awaited me at Saint Luke's with Malcolm.

When placed in this context, those glaring deficiencies in my ministry readiness portfolio didn't feel quite as disheartening. Drifting off to sleep, I resolved that this field education placement was worth my very best shot, regardless of how surreal and tenuous the ordination process might seem in the next several months. I slept well that night.

—

My Saint Luke's internship proved invaluable on many fronts. Feeling such a genuine sense of belonging with the church staff and the congregation, I wholeheartedly availed myself of the various learning opportunities afforded me. Although I was still struggling mightily in therapy with some powerful dysfunctional dynamics, my emerging identity as a soon-to-be-ordained-minister no longer felt so intimidating or bizarre.

One of my Emmanuel courses provided some excellent nuts and bolts information about the national church, conferences, presbyteries, and local congregations. However, my Saint Luke's internship gave me a practical perspective as to how formal church protocol actually played itself out within a congregation. Throughout my Saint Luke's experience, I was granted terrific access to such core congregational committees as the Official Board, the Session, Ministry and Personnel, Trustees, and Mission and Service.

While at Saint Luke's, I attended a weekly study group during the season of Advent and then led a similar kind of group during Lent. Listening to the participants intimately share how these sacred seasons in the church year intersected with their own lives deeply moved me. The manner in which they creatively integrated their own stories with the defining stories of their faith inspired me to do likewise.

I regularly visited parishioners in their own homes, nursing homes, and hospitals. The congregation was diverse in terms of age, color, education, financial resources, social standing, and sexual orientation. These intimate pastoral encounters taught me a great deal, invariably stretching me beyond the white, male, Anglo, straight, and middle-class lens through which I understood myself, others, and the world. Eventually, I also cottoned on to the fact that on these occasions, the parishioners in fact were doing most of the ministering.

Throughout my time at Saint Luke's, I frequently noted the congregation's consistent empathic response to individuals who regularly dropped by the church to solicit financial assistance. Many of those folks had been reduced to living on the remotest fringes of society as "street people" on account of their poverty, lack of education, serious mental health issues, color, and language. All too often these individuals had been treated by society as invisible and worthless. The Saint Luke's congregation was committed to doing their best to ensure that they felt noticed, appreciated, and welcomed.

Though I wasn't initially aware of it at the time, Saint Luke's was sowing the seeds of the "social gospel" within me. Having already theoretically learned this concept in seminary, I now began to understand how these words of Jesus from Matthew 25:35–40 were at the very heart of discipleship and ministry:

> "...for I was hungry and you gave me food, I was thirsty and you gave me drink, I was a stranger and you welcomed me, I was naked and you clothed me, I was sick and you visited me, I was in prison and you came to

me...truly, I say to you, as you did it to the least of my brethren, you did it to me."

Saint Luke's introduced me to the concept of "healing" and gave me a context in which to experience this often-understated aspect of mainstream Protestantism for myself. Following the regular worship service, about thirty folks usually showed up in the small chapel for the monthly healing service. This was a more intimate and personal service in which the predominant silence was only slightly broken by brief introductory scriptural statements and prayers.

During the service, individuals were invited to come forward one-by-one and kneel before the altar, where they received the "laying on of hands" and an accompanying blessing. For me, these services proved to be a great source of comfort by addressing my own pain and connecting me to others in their suffering, something I found particularly meaningful and uplifting.

Right from the beginning of my internship, I was given the opportunity to regularly participate in Sunday worship. My assignments ranged from reading scripture, composing and offering one of the prayers, meeting with the children before they left for their Sunday school classes, and even assisting Malcolm and the Session members with baptisms and communion.

On the last Sunday of my internship, sometime in April after Easter, I preached for the first time at Saint Luke's. In spite of hours of preparation, prayers, and sweat, I still felt extremely nervous. I was shaking so much that my knees kept hitting each other. Fortunately, the sides of the pulpit provided some ballast, the nervousness passed, and the sermon, "Beyond the Leper Colony," was delivered without incident. More importantly, this occasion gave me the opportunity to celebrate with my Saint Luke's friends and to thank them for their many kindnesses over the last several months.

However, Malcolm himself was the most valuable aspect of my entire experience at Saint Luke's. His non-judgmental and approachable demeanor, acute sensitivity to the needs and concerns of others, and pervasive "generosity of spirit" greatly touched me and countless others.

—

Intramural sports, especially hockey and flag football, were always an aspect of university life I had thoroughly enjoyed as a student at Queen's. In this regard, Emmanuel was no exception, yet there was one very significant difference. In principle, intramural sports teams were open to whoever wanted to participate, but as the goal of most intramural teams was still winning, usually those players with limited skills didn't get nearly as much playing time as more accomplished players. Moreover, they often only got to play in games when the outcome had been pretty much been decided.

At Emmanuel, we encouraged classmates to join our teams regardless of their ability or previous experience. We also made sure that everyone received about the same amount of actual playing time. Fortunately, there were a few of us with above-average ability and sports savvy, which helped our teams remain reasonably competitive. If we had focused primarily on winning by just utilizing our better players, our teams would have won several more games; however, making it possible for our less capable players to feel accepted and valued as full team members was far more gratifying. Seeing them psyched before games was always extra special.

By third year, our flag football team had progressed enough to be on the verge of qualifying for the playoffs. No small feat considering Emmanuel's inclusive approach to intramural sports. But if we didn't win our final regular season game, this exciting season would abruptly end.

Playing against a better team talent-wise, which had drastically underestimated us, we miraculously tied the score on the last play of the game; however, for a berth in the playoffs, a tie wouldn't suffice. We desperately needed the extra point.

With all of our best receivers covered, and just as someone was about to grab my flag and end the game, I spotted HIM. HE was very tall and gangly with long arms, giving HIM a huge wingspan. HE also had the least amount of football ability of anyone on the team. Yet at that critical moment, HE stood completely uncovered, hands at HIS sides, just over the goal line in the end zone.

Without really thinking, I threw a wobbly pass off my back foot in HIS general direction. The pass hung in the air forever until striking HIM squarely on HIS chest. With HIS hands still unbelievably at HIS sides, our season was a heartbeat away from ending. But as the football bounced back from HIS chest and headed towards the ground, HIS long arms suddenly reached out and pulled the football back to HIS chest.

For a moment, players on both teams were dumbfounded. HE grinned from ear to ear before being mobbed by jubilant teammates. By coming through with this catch for the ages, HE epitomized the longest of longshots beating the odds. Maybe there was hope for other long-shots. Maybe there was hope for me.

In spite of losing our next game and being eliminated from the play-offs, we savored a wonderful season. After the previous game's incredible come-from-behind victory, we all felt like champions!

—

While at Saint Luke's, I had the opportunity to visit a few parishio-ners both before and after their surgeries in some of the downtown general hospitals. Surprisingly, these visits weren't as intimidating for me as initially expected. Even so, I sensed that more pastoral experi-ence in a general hospital setting was needed before beginning my own parish ministry.

Another unit of Clinical Pastoral Education (CPE) that coming summer in a general hospital seemed like the best way to get the neces-sary pastoral training. Not wanting to repeat last year's late applications, I applied to three local CPE programs in mid-November. Two down-town general hospital programs soon granted me interviews, which at least from my perspective went quite well.

Although formally accepted in January by both of these excellent programs, I opted for the Toronto General Hospital, which happened to be the place of my birth. Within that same week, I also learned that my first semester's grades had set a new high-water mark for me. I imme-diately petitioned the Toronto Conference to grant me some extra time to take this second unit of CPE before officially beginning my ministry.

Thankfully, I was given permission to report for duty to somewhere not yet determined in late August, rather than in the more customary June or July.

—

Very early in the second semester, everyone in my class on the "ordination track" filled out the traditional forms that the national church's Settlement Committee would reference when deciding where newly ordained clergy would begin their respective ministries. There was a section on these forms for ordinands to list three geographical preferences, none of which were guaranteed, regarding their eventual placements. My colleagues and I knew that barring any extenuating family or health concerns, we could count on being assigned to multi-point pastoral charges composed of two to four small churches in very rural, sometimes remote, areas of the country.

As I regarded this section of the forms, no location preferences came to mind. I was single, healthy, and really didn't have any obligations that would prevent me from going anywhere in the country. The real issue for me revolved around where I felt called to serve. To help me with this discernment process, I made a point over the next few days to see if any clues popped up on the radar screen.

I soon recalled having seen a magazine cover a few weeks earlier while waiting to see my dentist. That particular cover, displaying an iconic scene of some fishing boats somewhere in the Maritimes, now prompted me to realize that I had been to every Canadian province except for those in the Maritimes: New Brunswick, Prince Edward Island, Nova Scotia, and Newfoundland. Going with my gut instinct, I listed the Maritimes as my first preference. There was no need to list anything else.

—

Sometime in the spring, I received a brief letter informing me about my placement: the Margaree Pastoral Charge in Cape Breton, Nova Scotia. This three-point pastoral charge included Calvin United Church in Margaree Harbour, Big Interval Church (summer only), and Wilson

United in Margaree Centre. Other than locating Margaree Harbour and Margaree Centre on a map, I knew nothing else about this area.

In fact, I really knew nothing about the Maritimes itself. I began second-guessing myself for having listed my preferred settlement location solely on a magazine cover. Yet my concerns were quickly put in perspective. Apparently, some of my colleagues couldn't even find their settlement placements on a map!

—

During the middle of my second semester, I met for the final time with the committee from the Toronto Conference, which had been overseeing my candidacy for ministry. Although somewhat anxious prior to the meeting, I felt resolved to make the best of things and let the chips fall where they may.

When all was said and done, the committee congratulated me and unanimously endorsed my candidacy. Leaving the meeting, my disbelief gave way to full-fledged gratitude. I celebrated with friends over great burgers, fries, and ginger ale.

—

Shortly thereafter came my fitting for a Geneva gown, which resembled those worn in worship services by the clergy at Timothy Eaton Memorial and Saint Luke's. While purchasing the gown, I also bought some long sleeve black clerical shirts, including the small white tabs which tucked into the front of each shirt's collar. I was able to try on samples of my gown and shirts to ensure that they fit properly. Gazing into a full-length mirror, I couldn't stifle an unanticipated chuckle. I was actually warming to who was looking back at me.

—

In third year, my interactions with peers and professors started to become more meaningful for me, as did the course work itself. During that year in particular, discussions with certain classmates in the student lounge and cafeteria played a pivotal role in helping me begin formulating my own opinions about a wide range of important issues. Topics such as biblical interpretation, theological beliefs, inclusive language, ordination of homosexuals, and women's reproductive rights were all fair grist for the mill.

Unlike most of my classmates, I didn't enter seminary with ardent, long-held opinions about these kinds of issues. This gave me more freedom to ponder without prejudice whatever was on the table and draw my own conclusions. I was also fortunate that the classmates with whom these passionate discussions took place often held positions considerably different from each other.

Such informal collegial exchanges helped me better grasp the actual issues than did classroom discussions, where usually some form of peer posturing took place. By the time third year ended, there was no mistaking the fact that I was definitely well left of center on all the hot-button issues.

—

Regretfully, in terms of actual learning, my cumulative classroom experience throughout seminary paled in comparison to what I had learned during the Saskatchewan summer internship, the unit of CPE, and the Saint Luke's field education placement. My capacity for critical thinking and theoretical discourse, though significantly improving, lacked the necessary adeptness to really take full advantage of what was available academically.

Yet there was still good reason to celebrate. I could feel my brain functioning better, firing on some long-lost circuits. My third year's B+ average certainly warranted another ginger ale toast with friends. Perhaps if another academic opportunity availed itself down the road, I'd be more capable from the get-go to put the pedal to the metal.

—

At the Emmanuel College Annual Dinner in late March, I was honored to receive the Sports Person of the Year Award. Although I'd received awards in first and second year as the hockey team's goalie and the football team's quarterback, this award put me over the moon. Throughout my life, sports had always provided me with a safe haven where I felt engaged, valued, and free.

My graduation on May 8, 1980 was somewhat bittersweet for me. As someone well acquainted with academic failure, I enjoyed the event's festive tone. Yet knowing that this was the last time we would be together as a class, I also felt some sadness. Depending on the locations of our future ministries, there was a high likelihood many of us would never see each other again.

A few days after receiving my Master of Divinity degree, I moved out of the Home and went to live with my friend Dave. He had an extra bedroom in his downtown apartment where I could live rent free until departing for Cape Breton in late August. Before leaving, I tearfully thanked the Home's residents and staff for their many kindnesses over the past year.

—

Most of the therapy with Dr. Smith in third year involved revisiting my childhood, teens, and early adulthood. I started to get a much better sense of how my parents' dynamics, both as individuals and as a couple, profoundly impacted me. I also faced the harsh truth that at the age of thirty-one, my level of emotional development in many ways was still stuck in adolescence.

With Dr. Smith's gentle nudging, delving deeper into my relationships with my mother and father over the next several months was both enlightening and arduous. While growing up, I had experienced my parents in radically different ways. Mom was always overly involved in my life, her presence at times consuming me. Dad, on the other hand, when he was at home, hardly engaged me at all. When my parents separated, I hadn't missed him.

In therapy I began to better understand some of my core psychopathology: fear of being consumed and fear of being abandoned. During childhood and adolescence, I must have unconsciously determined that relationships, especially those requiring any degree of intimacy and commitment, needed to be avoided at all costs. Although successful, this unconscious strategy unfortunately provided fertile soil for emotions such as self-loathing, rage, loneliness, and shame to grow deep roots and flourish.

As a result of such insights, I began to feel a greater affinity with my parents and how their respective backgrounds had unconsciously impacted them. Unlike me, they never had the benefit of therapeutic support to help identify and address some of their own dysfunctional issues. I began to cut them some slack and appreciate them more for who they were. Dr. Smith also helped me reflect about my lack of extended family members when I was growing up. An extended family could have provided me with different role models and frames of reference, especially in terms of relationships.

During my last few sessions with Dr. Smith, I focused on my upcoming ordination commitment. As a result of our sessions, I felt more capable in differentiating between past and present events and the various feelings they each evoked. This personal growth could help me develop the ability to get in touch with feelings such as anxiety and fear as they occurred and to react to them as an adult rather than as a child or teenager. When seen from this perspective, my ordination commitment didn't have to be experienced as an event that would consume me or usher in some other form of calamity.

In our last session, Dr. Smith and I both strongly agreed that additional therapy would help me build on my significant therapeutic gains. I thanked him for his invaluable support over the past sixteen months. Although still somewhat apprehensive, I wore less armor and sensed a brighter future awaited me.

Clinical Pastoral Education: Toronto General Hospital

Starting my second unit of CPE after graduating with a Master of Divinity degree one week earlier, I knew this experience was bound to enrich my professional expertise and provide me with some much-needed pastoral savvy in a general hospital setting. I also felt considerable anxiety reporting for duty on my first day.

During the next ten weeks, I knew that the program's curriculum, especially in the field of death and dying, was bound to test my mettle. I had never seen a corpse. I had never seen anyone close to death, let alone ministered to them or their loved ones. For that matter, I had never even attended a wake or a funeral.

Assuming responsibilities as a parish minister within weeks, I felt unsure and nervous about my ability to competently minister to folks in times of crisis. I hoped this unit of CPE would provide me with some hands-on experience and insights for such a core component of my imminent job description. Thankfully, some conscious breathing helped slow down my pulse as I stepped into the hospital on the program's first morning.

—

I had already met the program's supervisor, the Rev. Norm Headley, when interviewing for the program. He was an ordained minister in the United Church of Canada and had seemed very kind and knowledgeable. I was looking forward to learning from him and hoped that my peers would engender a similar feeling.

We spent half of the morning sharing some of our backgrounds with each other. All of my peers had completed their first or second year of seminary. Just like me last year, they were taking their first unit of CPE in order to comply with their respective denominational requirements for ordination. One man was Korean, and the other two women and two men were Caucasian. They were all Protestant: two Episcopalians, one Baptist, one Presbyterian, and one United Church of Canada. Age-wise, all of us, including Norm, were probably within ten years of each other.

—

After a mid-morning coffee break, it was time for a tour of the hospital. We picked up our "Chaplain Intern" name badges and official chaplaincy attire: white lab coats. While we were garbing up, some spontaneous references to Dr. Kildare, Groucho Marx, and penguins provided some nice group levity.

The hospital was a composite of several large buildings, or wings, connected by countless corridors. Even though there were plenty of color-coded lines and arrows to assist with directions, I felt totally disoriented shortly after the tour started. After about ninety minutes, our supervisor mercifully ended the tour by showing us the piece de resistance: the small furnished bedroom the hospital provided for the on-call chaplain.

Many aspects of CPE are quite similar regardless of the site; however, the respective programs at the Toronto General Hospital and the Whitby Psychiatric Hospital had one very significant difference. Whereas the latter only required students to equally share the rotating leadership for the hospital's regular Sunday worship services, the former required students to equally share the pastoral care department's on-call responsibility: weeknights from eight o'clock in the evening until eight o'clock in the morning and on weekends from eight o'clock in the morning until eight o'clock in the evening and also from eight o'clock in the evening until eight o'clock in the morning.

Aside from providing the on-call chaplain with a small bedroom, the hospital even threw in free vouchers for supper and breakfast. The on-call chaplain also received two different-colored pagers, which had to be carried at all times. One pager was used exclusively for situations needing an immediate response, such as "Code Blue" (resuscitation team), or a call to the Emergency Room to help with a crisis. The other pager conveyed less urgent yet important pastoral requests.

Like me, the rest of the students already knew about this on-call component from when we initially interviewed for the program, but now this aspect of the program, especially the pager requiring an immediate response, seemed almost ominous. Fortunately, lunch provided us with a much-needed opportunity to quell some of our mutual performance anxiety.

After lunch, our supervisor gave us a detailed outline about the program itself, as well as our primary "floor" assignments. Norm had remembered my hope to learn more about ministry in times of death, dying, grief, and loss. I was assigned to "Oncology."

While riding the subway back to Dave's at the end of that first day, I began having second thoughts about taking this non-mandatory second unit of CPE. Why wasn't I leaving for a pastoral charge in June, like most of my peers? Deep down, though, I knew that some general hospital experience was essential before beginning my Cape Breton ministry

—

The first two weeks passed reasonably smoothly as I eased into my role as a member of the oncology team. I felt warmly received by most everyone and soon began to get the lay of the land. Previous pastoral visitation experiences at Saint Luke's Church and the Whitby Psychiatric Hospital helped me to get my sea-legs much quicker than anticipated, and also minimized initial feelings of anxiety and self-consciousness.

During week three of the program, however, my energy was directed elsewhere. I primarily focused on Tuesday night's ordination service and then my preaching debut as a newly ordained minister at Sunday morning's service at Timothy Eaton Memorial. My peers graciously shifted their own on-call responsibilities to free me from any extra duties during this special week.

Ordination

On the morning of my ordination, I felt very good about the emotional developmental gains which therapy with Dr. Smith had made possible; however, I was also aware that in spite of such recent personal growth, my ordination service might cause me considerable anxiety. Nonetheless, I still felt undeterred in trusting the incredible restorative process that, in less than four years, had brought me to this point.

This evening I would formally step forward as a disciple of Jesus and profess my vocation as an ordained minister under the auspices of the United Church of Canada. Sensing that a reality check still seemed warranted, I put on my clerical shirt, attached the white tab under the front collar, and donned my black gown along with the Master of Divinity academic hood. Game on!

—

This year the Toronto Conference had arranged for the service to take place in the small city of Barrie, which was about a one-hour drive north of the Toronto. In doing so, the conference wished to affirm the valuable ministries of those many surrounding smaller rural churches. With twenty-eight candidates involved in the service, no local United Church building could accommodate the large number of conference officers, other church personnel, and also the candidates' families and friends who would be attending. St. Mary's Roman Catholic Church, the only church in the area that could seat everyone, had generously offered to host the event.

I was glad that my friends Dave, Jerry Pernu from Sudbury, and his wife, Diane, would be there to support me. Although each of these friends had seen me at my very worst, our friendships over the years remained remarkably intact. Also joining us was my former fiancée, Helen P. Her willingness to attend was extra special considering what we'd been through together.

Both Stephen Mabee from Timothy Eaton Memorial and Malcolm Finlay from Saint Luke's had graciously agreed to lay hands on me when it was my turn to be ordained. Each of these two men and their respective churches had played pivotal roles in helping to make this occasion possible. Their attendance meant a great deal to me.

—

Since none of us owned a car, Dave agreed to pick up a rental. He had recently seen an eye-catching advertisement for "Rent-A-Wreck." This company's rental cars were all weary road warriors whose prime years had long since disappeared; however, these drivable wrecks were also much cheaper.

With money being tight for both of us at the time, we opted to take our chances with a wreck. The thought of me arriving in a "wreck" for my ordination service seemed so full of comedic irony that we immediately burst into wails of laughter. Later in the afternoon, Dave and I, along with Jerry, Diane, and Helen piled into what drove like an old barge.

We planned to arrive at the church no later than seven o'clock, which would allow time for me to join my colleagues for some mutual support before the seven-thirty big event. Our commute was filled with lots of playful reminiscences, banter, and laughter until we encountered some unexpected heavy Tuesday night traffic. Expletives soon laced our discourse.

We soon ditched our plans for an early arrival and now desperately hoped to just get there before the service started. Fortunately, the traffic eventually cleared, allowing me to madly dash into the church with less than ten minutes to spare. I joined my colleagues and just managed to don my clerical duds before the service commenced.

—

After we had all lined up and began to enter the sanctuary, the hymn "Praise to the Lord, the Almighty" officially opened the service. This hymn had always been one of my long-time favorites, yet hearing the words sung that night by hundreds of attendees, accompanied by a massive choir, a fantastic organ, and several brass instruments, sent my soul soaring. Although each candidate had been given a hymn book beforehand, I was too overcome with emotion to join in the singing.

Once the hymn ended and everyone sat down, I looked around the sanctuary. The place was packed. With every seat taken, a large number of people were standing at the back and along the sides of the sanctuary. The chancel area and several front pews were awash with colors from the gowns, academic hoods, and liturgical stoles of the many clergy and academics in attendance.

—

As the service moved along, I continued to feel reasonably calm, except for some surges of adrenalin, which seemed quite normal given the circumstances. I found these verses in the first scripture lesson from Isaiah to be particularly powerful, dramatically setting the stage for what would soon be taking place.

> And I said: "Woe is me! For I am lost; for I am a man of unclean lips, and I dwell in the midst of a people of unclean lips; for my eyes have seen the King, the Lord of hosts!" Then flew one of the seraphim to me, having in his hand a burning coal which he had taken with tongs from the altar. And he touched my mouth, and said: "Behold, this has touched your lips; your guilt is taken away, and your sin forgiven." And I heard the voice of the Lord saying, "Whom shall I send, and who will go for us?" Then I said, "Here am I! Send me."
>
> Isaiah 6:5–8

I had already heard this text a few times over the past three years, but that night I seemed to be hearing these words for the very first time. Like Isaiah, I too would soon step forth and express my willingness to serve.

The Gospel reading also conveyed a transcendent, exhilarating clarity in preparing me to receive my commissioning as a disciple of Jesus Christ.

> And Jesus came and said to them, "All authority in heaven and on earth has been given to me. Go therefore and make disciples of all nations, baptizing them in the name of the Father and of the Son and of the Holy

Spirit, teaching them to observe all that I have commanded you; and lo, I am with you always, to the close of the age."

Matthew 28:18–20

The phrase "I am with you always" was particularly poignant. Without this kind of reassurance, there's no way I would have been there in the first place, let alone heading off to Nova Scotia within three months as an ordained minister. For me, Jesus' presence in my life was an eternal, immutable game-changer.

—

Finally, the time came when each of the candidates would in turn step forward and formally accept their call. There were nineteen candidates ahead of me. I felt ready. But waves of panic suddenly started sweeping over me as the names were called. Remembering to breathe, I tried to stay grounded. I reminded myself that old childhood fears of being consumed by commitments were fueling the trauma rather than the ordination commitment itself. I tried convincing myself that now, as an adult, previous emotional survival strategies such as running away from obligations were no longer necessary.

Yet my panic continued to strengthen, seemingly becoming stronger every few seconds. Soon it was the most horrifying panic attack I'd ever experienced. Fearing that even the slightest movement on my part could cause me to completely fly apart, I sat perfectly still. Gripping my knees firmly, I kept my head down and continued to breathe.

I was in grave distress. Keeping track of those ahead of me in the queue ceased to matter. Standing up, let alone walking up the aisle, was now totally out of the question. Ordination was not in the cards for me that night. I sensed the opportunity was lost forever. Woe is me! I was flawed and had over-reached.

Like Paul in his letter to the Romans, I frantically clung to the hope that nothing could ever separate me from the love of God in Christ Jesus my Lord. When the candidate next to me stood up and walked to the center aisle, I knew my name would be called momentarily. An ominous future loomed.

—

Yet within seconds, the powerful panic attack suddenly began subsiding. Calmness quickly started to envelope me. In fact, this fortuitous turn of events was so rapid and unexpected that I was afraid to believe it was happening. Without even noticing that the previous candidate was already walking back to his seat, I heard my name called: Gordon Douglas Postill. I took a deep breath and lifted my head. Seraphic support lifted me out of the pew, escorted me up the aisle, and empowered me to make the commitment I no longer feared.

While making my ordination vows, everything seemed to slow down. Jesus' words, "I am with you always, to the close of the age" grounded me. Never had things seemed so right.

After kneeling for the laying on of hands, I rose for one final blessing. I felt deeply humbled and completely at ease. While walking back down the aisle, this ecstatic longshot barely resisted thrusting his arms straight up to the heavens. Touchdown! Without any forethought, I suddenly decided to adapt the prophet Isaiah's powerful declaration of faith (Isaiah 6:8) to form my own faith-based mantra: "Here am I, my Lord Jesus! Send me."

—

Following the service, I mingled with some of my classmates and church officials. I specifically sought out Malcolm and Stephen to thank them for having made the trip to formally share in my ordination. I was then able to join my friends. Immediately after the service, Dave took my picture, capturing unbridled joy and overflowing gratitude.

Preaching at Timothy Eaton Memorial Church

I thoroughly enjoyed returning to Toronto with my friends after the ordination service, yet before going to sleep that night, more anxiety arrived. As adrenalin coursed through my veins, post-ordination basking quickly took a back seat to what Sunday morning had in store for me.

Clergy within the United Church of Canada traditionally preached their first sermon as an ordained minister in the church that endorsed their candidacy. This meant that within five days, I'd be preaching at Timothy Eaton Memorial Church. With barely enough time to catch my breath after such a profound ordination experience, I now prepared for another event that was also bound to be right up there on the profundity scale.

The day after my ordination, euphoria yielded to exhaustion. I was totally depleted. I hoped that time could somehow slow down enough for me to recoup some energy. Then suddenly, ready or not, Sunday morning arrived and found me standing alone on the sidewalk in front of Timothy Eaton Memorial about forty-five minutes before the service started.

I remembered standing on that same patch of sidewalk less than three years earlier. At that time, with my highly questionable past and suspect character, I faced the daunting and seemingly impossible task of finding a congregation to endorse me as a candidate for ministry. Yet now I stood on that same patch of sidewalk as a newly ordained minister, all collared-up with my Geneva gown and academic hood under my arm.

—

Suddenly, my eyes caught sight of the large sign on the church's front lawn and I read the words: 11 AM "Beyond the Leper Colony" (Guest Preacher) Rev. Gordon Postill and 7 PM "The Parable of the Assassin" Rev. Stanford Lucyk. Receiving twin billing with Stan, one of the United Church of Canada's most renowned preachers and a key mentor of mine, made this occasion even more special.

Since Stan had arrived at Timothy Eaton Memorial as the new senior minister while I was still on my Saskatchewan summer internship in 1978, we didn't meet each other until my return to Toronto. During my second year at Emmanuel, I spent my Sunday mornings with the church's youth group and then with Saint Luke's United Church on Sunday mornings in my third year. As a result, I could only hear Stan preach on Sunday evening.

After attending two of these evening services in the fall of 1978, I was hooked. Right up until leaving for my own pastoral charge in late August 1980, I rarely missed an opportunity to learn from this "preaching maven." Stan's sermons were consistently filled with astonishing biblical insights, making even the most familiar scripture passages more meaningful and provocative.

No one could ever listen to Stan's sermons without perceiving the amount of disciplined scholarship and due diligence he always brought to his craft. Like many people, I considered Stan to be both an outstanding preacher as well as a tremendous teacher. Moreover, Stan's bearing, especially during worship, conveyed a sense of "gravitas," which I found very appealing.

—

After slipping into my gown and attaching the academic hood, I joined Stan and the choir for a prayer. I could feel my eyes tearing up as everyone extended their congratulations and best wishes. We then gathered in the narthex at the rear of the sanctuary and proceeded to queue up in pairs for the processional hymn.

All of a sudden, the powerful church organ majestically called us to worship. As the choir began their slow processional up the middle aisle to the chancel, their voices were quickly joined by those of the congregation. The magnificent opening hymn, "Holy, Holy, Holy, Lord God Almighty," immediately flooded me with emotion. Following the last pair of choir members, Stan and I entered the sanctuary and started processing up what seemed like a never-ending aisle.

I began feeling light-headed and flushed. My hands were shaking so much that I feared my open hymn book could become airborne at any second. After reaching my seat and settling down somewhat, I marveled at this mind-blowing start to my ministry. Here I was preaching at Timothy Eaton Memorial Church to a packed congregation, as well as to many others in metropolitan Toronto via the live radio broadcast on the radio station 1540 CHIN.

—

Eventually, my time to preach arrived. Anxiety and adrenalin co-mingled as I climbed into the pulpit. Gazing out at the very large congregation, I totally forgot my opening remarks. Mercifully, my primary mantra, "Here am I, my Lord Jesus! Send me," quickly came to mind and helped me regain some composure.

First and foremost, I expressed my deep gratitude to the congregation for having endorsed this longshot's candidacy for ordained ministry. Without their support and trust, this moment would never have been conceivable, let alone possible. I would forever be in their debt.

I had revised my Saint Luke's sermon, "Beyond the Leper Colony," and still used Luke 5:12–16 as the primary exegetical text. While contextualizing our unique journeys from brokenness to wholeness, I underscored the hope and healing which Grace offers us. To my complete surprise while preaching, whenever ominous waves of anxiety seemed ready to overwhelm me, a newfound sense of "pulpit belonging" kept such threats at bay.

—

The rest of the service flew by. After offering the benediction, I joined Stan for the recessional. Unlike my earlier walk up the aisle, exuberance now replaced anxiety. Walking past the pew where some of my friends were standing, I took extra delight in seeing them smiling and nodding approvingly. Still too emotional to sing, I was in no hurry for this walk to end.

Once we reached the narthex, Stan offered his congratulations, as did Charlie Plaskett, Stephen Mabee, and Pat MacKay. The entire staff of Timothy Eaton Memorial Church had been wonderful advocates, mentors, and friends for me over the past three years. I was going to miss them.

Many parishioners expressed their appreciation for my sermon. Some of them told me how it had specifically spoken to them. My eyes welled up when Malcolm and his family came over to offer their congratulations. I was particularly delighted to embrace Helen. The fact that she had attended both my ordination in Barrie and then this service as well made both events even more memorable for me.

Finally, I hugged some longtime friends who were there to support me: Dave, my dear childhood friend; Robin Parke and his wife, Jane; and my high school buddy, Jim Dickinson, with his girlfriend, Annette. To cap off this truly marvelous day, Robin and Jane had invited us back to their home. While Annette helped Jane put the finishing touches on a sumptuous roast beef dinner with all the trimmings, the "boys" played outside with a nerf ball in the backyard. As we bantered back and forth with each other as usual, nothing appeared to have changed. Yet we all knew differently.

With my buddies Dave, Jim, and Robin

Clinical Pastoral Education (cont'd)

Less than a week after my ordination and subsequent preaching engagement at Timothy Eaton Memorial Church, CPE officially began for me in earnest. While on-call, I awoke to the piercing sound of the immediate response pager at three o'clock in the morning. This was the first time I'd been paged in the middle of the night.

Without having much time to think, I called the number indicated on the pager. Once informed where to report, I quickly dressed and hurried to the appropriate nursing station. The staff immediately brought me up to speed with what was happening and how I could help.

—

A seventy-one-year-old Hispanic woman had just died of complications from a recent surgery for metastatic lung cancer. Although a Catholic priest had given the woman the Last Rites about an hour before her death, the staff thought the family would benefit from some additional pastoral care before the patient's body was removed. No textbook could have prepared me or my Anglo sense of public propriety for what I was about to experience.

Although I knocked on the door before entering, no one appeared to see me. Three women were draped across the deceased's bed, and a younger woman was actually lying under the covers and kissing the dead woman's face. Three men, one of whom was much older, were standing over in the far corner.

The three women were crying. The younger woman was sobbing uncontrollably. Even though words were scarce, I heard both English and Spanish being spoken.

I stood still, breathed, and held the family in prayer. My gut told me to just stand quietly on the periphery. One of my favorite mantras, "Be still and know that I am God," helped ground me. After I had been standing just inside the room for a minute or two, one of the men came over to me.

Upon hearing that I was a chaplain, he told me that his mother had just died. He then introduced me to his siblings and to his father. Apparently, the women still draped over the deceased's body were her daughters. The young woman lying under the covers was one of the deceased's granddaughters.

My words of sympathy and support were in turn translated for those who only spoke Spanish. I stood with them quietly around the bedside for a few minutes. When the loud sobbing subsided, I offered to pray with them. Although the granddaughter continued to lie under the covers, the rest of us joined hands and prayed together. Some of the family prayed the "Our Father" in English with me while others prayed in Spanish. We wept. We hugged.

Later, as I prepared to leave, many of the family members thanked me in English and Spanish for my support. In response, I expressed appreciation for having shared such a sacred time with them. At the nursing station, the staff thanked me, saying that I was now "one of their own."

—

Returning to the chaplain's room, I reflected on what had just happened. Prior to this visit, I had never pastorally intervened in situations where death was involved, where people were acutely suffering, or where a language other than English was spoken. Yet suddenly I found myself weeping uncontrollably. Unlike the young woman in the visit who was deeply grieving her grandmother, I never had the chance to even meet any of my grandparents before they died.

Earlier internships over the past three years had certainly affirmed my pastoral potential and personable manner. Yet lying on the bed, I had a hunch that there was something more about this visit that needed further mining. Within the next couple of days, I presented this case in my next verbatim.

The depth of the verbatim process itself, including input from my supervisor and peers, enabled me to understand how this particular visit could very well have marked my ministerial "coming of age." Whereas the ordination service confirmed my call to ministry, this visit confirmed my ability to minister.

From that moment on, I didn't feel nearly as apprehensive about those steep professional learning curves awaiting me in Cape Breton. With less to fear, I had more energy and confidence for making the most of the program's remaining six weeks. Here am I, my Lord Jesus! Send me.

—

About a week later, my peers and I were given the opportunity to observe an actual surgery from inside the operating room. Like everyone else, I signed up, and within days we received our respective surgery assignments as well as brief descriptions about them.

I was slated to observe a Whipple procedure, a very complicated and risky surgery, lasting several hours. This operation is usually performed to remove cancerous tumors in the pancreas, and often involves other organs, such as the gallbladder, duodenum, and the stomach. Once this information started to sink in, I would have gladly bailed if given half the chance

I met the medical team at the appointed hour. Scrubbing up with them and donning the usual surgical garb seemed totally surreal. Some of the surgical team members encouraged me to leave at any time during the operation if I began to feel uncomfortable. The surgeon even added that he and countless others had all made at least one quick exit from an operating room during their early medical training.

Upon entering the operating room, where a man in his fifties had already been prepped and sedated for his surgery, I was instructed to stand next to the anesthesiologist near the patient's head. Someone on the surgical team jokingly instructed me to fall away from the patient rather than on top of him if I should faint.

I felt surprisingly calm until the first incision was made down the center of the man's chest. Seeing the patient's blood emerge, I quickly began to feel nauseous and light-headed. Although on the verge of leaving the operating room, I somehow managed to regain my composure.

The surgical team's collaborative expertise was awesome to behold. The surgery itself was very complex, intricate, and risky. There was a lot of blood. Even though everyone was focused on the arduous and delicate tasks at hand, they also seemed to savor their craft and camaraderie.

I was so enthralled by their teamwork that time for me flew by almost unnoticed. Hours later, the patient was on his way to the recovery room. The team agreed that given the patient's advanced disease progression, the surgery couldn't have been more successful. They congratulated each other for a job well done. They even lauded me for hanging in there with them to the end.

From my perspective, the surgical team members had all been magnificent. Having just witnessed this truly remarkable display of professionals at the top of their game, I felt motivated to pursue my own vocational excellence. For the remainder of the program, I availed myself of whatever learning opportunities crossed my path.

—

As the CPE program wound down, I felt good about having accomplished my initial learning objectives. A general hospital's environment now seemed much less intimidating for me. I felt more confident that my current pastoral skills would pass muster in Cape Breton; however, with the help of my supervisor and peers, I sensed that something of far greater consequence had been happening to me over the past ten weeks.

My ability to be emotionally and spiritually present with those to whom I was ministering had increased significantly. I felt more capable in spontaneously and authentically engaging others without my previous level of fear about intimacy and transparency. Although additional personal and professional development in these areas was indeed warranted in the future, I felt confident in taking off my pastoral training wheels.

The patients and their families, the hospital staff, Norm, and my peers all played significant roles in making this program such a dynamic and timely learning experience for me. My peer relationships were among the many highlights. Although we shared some very intense periods of conflict, my peer relationships were much less strained than those from a year ago. In many ways, my peers this year shared many similarities with last year's group. Yet this time round, I was different.

Mom

One week before leaving for Cape Breton, I attempted to reconcile with my mother. During my time in seminary, our relationship had become increasingly strained. For most of my adult life, I had turned to Mom whenever I found myself in this or that dire predicament. She had always come through for me. Yet now that I was finally becoming responsible and finding my way in the world, Mom felt left behind.

Her attitude was confusing and pissed me off. Just days before my ordination service and the Timothy Eaton Memorial preaching engagement, we had unleashed our respective resentments. Harsh and condemnatory words toward each other were spoken. As a result, Mom chose not to attend either event. I felt relieved.

In this last visit before leaving for Cape Breton, I wanted to tell my mother that her selfless support over the years would always be appreciated and never forgotten. I wanted to reaffirm my love for her. I also wanted her blessing. However, immediately upon my arrival, I knew that any form of reconciliation between us was out of the question. Mom was hurt and angry. I soon became hurt and angry. We barely engaged each other.

To our credit, the visit ended without another major blowout. Knowing ahead of time that our relationship was complicated, I wasn't surprised by the visit's outcome. Yet I still felt sad. I hoped at some point down the road we could resolve at least some of our differences. As for now, I had a plane to catch.

Cape Breton Bound

After a great send-off with friends, I boarded a direct flight to Sydney, Nova Scotia, where some parishioners would be waiting to drive me to beautiful Margaree. Once the flight reached its cruising altitude, my first thoughts were, *Holy shit! This is really happening!* I was now on the threshold of reporting for duty as an ordained minister in the United Church of Canada! Buoyant amazement enveloped me as I reflected on this past decade's astonishing ride.

Then suddenly out of nowhere, a chilling reality check got in my face and demanded an audience. My friends, though now fully on board with their support, had all candidly shared that they wouldn't be surprised if I got booted out of the ministry within a year as a result of some reckless personal indiscretion or drunken expletive-laced rant. In my heart of hearts, I knew they were right. There was still so much about me that required major restoration.

Without a strong commitment to continue my personal growth, longstanding destructive proclivities, though having lost some of their footing, were still very close at hand. If left unattended, they would most certainly dash my fervent hopes for a meaningful life and a faithful ministry. Not unlike that earlier crucial decision to quit drinking alcohol in January 1978, I felt a similar prescience in vowing to continue my restorative process for however long it should take.

Eventually, I stopped reflecting. For the rest of the flight, this grateful longshot just stared out the window, seeing nothing but deep blue sky without an ice floe in sight.

August 2013
Duxbury, Massachusetts

EPILOGUE

In the early fall of 1980 after I had recently begun my ministry, Maureen Scobie, a freelance journalist from Toronto, was visiting in the area and happened to attend one of our worship services. Afterward, she asked to interview me for what she thought might make a good human-interest story. Sure enough, Maureen's full-page article, "Gordon Postill: From the Pits to the Promise," was published in the February 1981 edition of the *United Church Observer* magazine. My parishioners, Maureen, and I were all chuffed!

About a month later, I received a totally unexpected call from Helen T, my former great love at Queen's University who had abruptly ditched me in May 1969 with a "Dear John" letter. She had come across this very same article completely by chance and wanted to offer her congratulations. Helen felt astounded that I had become an ordained minister and was glad that my fortunes had changed. She was also happily married.

Since I was flying to Toronto in the near future and serendipitously changing planes in her city, we agreed to continue our endearing conversation in person during my one-hour layover between flights. A few weeks later upon entering the airport, I easily spotted Helen who was still a knockout! We fondly reminisced about the joys of our relationship as well as the regrets. After hearing my flight's final boarding call, we amicably parted, albeit with a wispy sadness on my part for what might have been, and bid adieu to our intoxicating interlude from years ago.

—

A few months later, Robin Young and I met on Evans Beach near Margaree Harbour in the summer of 1981. She and her sister Candy had driven up from Boston and were touring the Maritimes. Having been the minister of the Margaree Pastoral Charge since August 1980 and still single, I was faithfully attending to my "beach" ministry.

I readily struck up a conversation with Robin and Candy, thoroughly enjoying their company for about an hour before they had to continue their trip. Although the chances of ever seeing them again were slim, my gut instinct prompted me to get their addresses. After Robin responded to my Christmas card, subsequent letters and phone conversations ultimately compelled me to drive to Boston in June 1982 for a visit.

As I crossed the border, a US Immigration Officer asked me how long I planned to be in the States. I said that depending on how things went that night, he would either see me the next day or in two weeks.

After our first night together, I was utterly smitten. Too bad I didn't get to see that same US Immigration Officer when I crossed back over the border two weeks later! Most fittingly, Stan Lucyk married us at Timothy Eaton Memorial Church less than a year later on April 16, 1983.

Having taken a leave of absence from her job, Robin was thankfully able to join me for my last two months in beautiful Margaree. My parishioners delighted in our happiness, giving us a heart-warming wedding reception and then, just a few weeks later, a very generous send-off for the ages.

—

During that third and final year in Cape Breton before moving to Boston with Robin, I knew my personal growth and professional development were stalling and needed tending. This also felt like the right time to stop smoking weed and become completely clean. Over the next decade, extensive psychotherapy, three advanced units of CPE, a Doctor of Ministry program from Boston University, contemplative prayer, and long distance running helped me immensely. Although so vitally important throughout our marriage, Robin's love, integrity, and wisdom were particularly crucial in this period while I was still getting my shit together.

I'm especially grateful that my dad and mom, though still separated and living in different cities, on several occasions were able to see me happily married and professionally thriving before their respective deaths in 1993 and 1996. Shortly after beginning my ministry in Margaree, I had thankfully reconnected with my sister Louise, who was married and living in Montreal. Despite living considerable distances away from Louise and her family, Robin and I have always enjoyed visits with them every several years.

—

I had the privilege and honor of serving congregations in Nova Scotia and Ontario prior to moving on Easter Monday 1991 with Robin, a US citizen, to warmer climes in Naples, Florida, where we'd vacationed a year earlier. The fact that we didn't have employment waiting for us didn't thwart our enthusiasm for this audacious adventure.

Two months after arriving in Naples, I serendipitously learned of a local hospice chaplaincy position soon becoming available. The rest is history. I would go on to spend the last twenty-four years of my ministry providing spiritual care to hospice patients and their families in Florida and Massachusetts. As a chaplain, I realized an important profes-sional goal by becoming "Board Certified" through the Association of Professional Chaplains (APC) in 1997 and then later served as APC's State Representative of Massachusetts from 2002–2006.

During my ministry, I was fortunate to acquire considerable expertise in the areas of Critical Incident Stress Management (CISM) and end-of-life health care ethics. After the terrorist attacks on 9-11-2001, I had the honor in March 2002 to lead a CISM team from Naples, Florida to New York City to provide a week of support for NYPD personnel. I was also privileged to serve for ten years as the ethics committee chair of the Hospice & Palliative Care Federation of Massachusetts and offered ethics workshops throughout MA.

—

I feel grateful and humbled that over the years most people told me how much they felt at ease with me and found my ministry beneficial, an outcome that occasionally surprised those who weren't anticipating much of a benefit in the first place. More often than not, pastoral visits in particular invariably left me with an unmistakable sense of also having been a recipient of whatever "ministering" had just taken place. For me, this edifying reciprocity never got old.

I consider myself deeply blessed for having had the enriching and fulfilling opportunities my "call to ministry" in 1976 continually afforded me. The ready access that folks granted me and the high degree of transparency with which they shared their life stories, often at their most vulnerable, I constantly cherished. In no small measure those entrusted to my pastoral care have been my greatest teachers about what really matters. I am forever in their debt.

—

In 1977, Timothy Eaton Memorial Church took a chance on me as a candidate for ordained ministry when I could have only been described as a longshot at best. I am eternally grateful to this congregation. Being invited back in January 2006 as a guest preacher to celebrate the twenty-fifth anniversary of my ordination is one of my life's most treasured highlights, especially since I was able to share it with Robin, longtime friends, some former parishioners from St. Andrew's United Church in Oshawa, and also my esteemed mentors, Malcolm Finlay and Stan Lucyk.

I was particularly delighted to see Helen P and talk with her after the service. We had reconnected as friends in the late eighties and used to meet every two to three years for lunch whenever I came to Toronto. During one of our visits, Helen shared how she had actually been planning on breaking up with me in April 1979 and regretted that I had pulled the trigger first. Sadly, Helen died in 2007. She holds a special place in my heart forever.

—

Ever since my 1978 summer mission field experience in Saskatchewan, gratitude quickly overwhelms me whenever I attempt to sing the first verse of John Newton's hymn "Amazing Grace." May this heartfelt reaction never change!

Amazing grace! How sweet the sound,
That saved a wretch like me!
I once was lost, but now am found;
Was blind, but now I see.

Over the last several years, I've become more comfortable in my own skin while also doubling down on paying my many blessings forward. Even so, occasionally, in response to a perceived slight by a complete stranger, I can find myself suddenly spewing expletives while quickly donning armor for combat. Apparently my longstanding quest for emotional sobriety is far from finished.

Whenever I've periodically looked back over my life, that astonishing "ice floes to ordination" decade in particular evokes feelings such as hope, validation, courage, and gratitude. For me, especially in recent years, feelings like these have never been more important.

—

During the first few years of married life, Robin and I kept our options open regarding children, but it eventually became apparent that by making our marriage and careers the first and second priorities respectively, we felt fulfilled, content, and happy. Though it sounds cliché, we quickly became and have remained each other's best friend, thoroughly enjoying our own company, whether hiking the National Parks or Swiss Alps, strolling the Seine or Charles River Esplanade, relating events from our jobs over supper, or sharing quiet time together reading. In spite of rare patches of discord over the years, we have been well-suited, totally committed, and deeply in love. The enriching addition of indoor cats several years ago to our self-contained lifestyle has provided us with constant entertainment, affection, and occasional aggravation!

In February 2015, after Robin had been experiencing some difficulty concentrating as well as occasional memory lapses for about a year, we decided she should take a few months off to get recharged from her many fulfilling yet demanding jobs over the years. Accordingly, Robin informed her employer about this intention and in April resigned from her senior social work manager position. But when a six-month "sabbatical" did nothing to help resolve her increasing cognitive difficulties, Robin finally agreed that it was time for us to meet with a neurologist. To completely focus my attention and energy on the home front for whatever formidable challenges probably lay ahead of us, I retired at the end of November after thirty-five years of ministry.

Heartbreakingly in early February 2016, after a series of tests, Robin at age sixty-two was diagnosed with "primary progressive aphasia," which is a rare type of frontotemporal dementia. Such nightmarish news cut us to the quick. Shortly thereafter, while we were sitting in our living room, Robin turned to me and with her voice quivering pleaded, "I don't want to wither." From that moment, helping Robin to live as normally, fully, contentedly, and safely for as long as possible has been my sole objective. In January 2019, Robin's diagnosis was changed to "early-onset Alzheimer's disease." Yet this merely meant swapping nightmares.

Swiss Alps hiking break in Zermatt 2017 (our last trip)

Robin's courage, resilience, and graceful demeanor, amiably allowing me to increasingly micro-manage her activities such as getting dressed, have thus far enabled us to keep our chins above the waterline. Support from family, friends, and former colleagues has helped us considerably. In particular, assistance from Robin's sister, Candy, and brother-in-law, Glenn, who live nearby, has been invaluable. Periodic support from a psychologist has also greatly benefited me whenever I've felt overwhelmed and adrift.

Given our respective professions, we've had many discussions about what to do in this kind of heart-wrenching situation. Our respective wishes in this regard were always similar: remaining safely at home for a long as possible, placement in a memory care unit when professional assistance was required and ensuring that the "partner-caregiver" received the necessary respite to get recharged.

Over the past six years, Robin and I have shed many tears, experienced considerable anguish, felt our lives ransacked on numerous fronts by Alzheimer's relentless onslaught, and known more horrors await. Despite the agonizing, staggering, and daunting impact of Robin's ruthless disease progression on each of us and our relationship, we still approach every day with the attitude of finding as much delight and solace as possible. Withstanding those inevitable, extra-challenging stretches for me has become more a matter of taking "one breath at a time" rather than "one day at a time." Earlier this year, we celebrated our thirty-seventh wedding anniversary. I'm still smitten by my beloved Robin, the love of my life.

A crucial godsend for me ever since Robin's diagnosis has been the almost constant conviction that much of my overall life experience, both personally and professionally, has been instilling in me the wherewithal necessary for this ultimate ministry, mindfully and lovingly ensuring that both of us receive the care and support we need. With Robin's dementia accelerating, such conviction helped me to make the gut-wrenching yet absolutely necessary decision for us to move as soon as there is a vacancy (we are next on the waiting list) to a highly reputable senior living community that offers both an "independent living" apartment for me as well as "memory care" accommodation for Robin. We can also bring our cats, Callie and Joey, as well as remain in Boston.

Of utmost importance to me is that by living in this kind of community, once COVID-19 is no longer a threat, I can easily visit Robin each day and bring her to my digs to hang out together with Callie and Joey. I shall also be able to take her outside for short walks on lovely adjacent wooded trails. With professionals attending to most of Robin's care, I can focus more on being her husband and also attend to those aspects of myself that, out of necessity, have been put on hold. Most of all, I fervently pray that Robin's current life expectancy of about three years allows for at least a few more months, or perhaps even a year, in which she can truly enjoy some aspects of each day before Alzheimer's inevitably engulfs her.

With enormous heart-rending, unnerving personal changes looming for us, especially for Robin, it is no wonder that to stay focused and fortified, not unlike a certain ministerial longshot going forth in faith forty years earlier, I turn to my long-treasured mantra, "Here am I, my Lord Jesus! Send me."

October 2020
Boston, Massachusetts

CPSIA information can be obtained
at www.ICGtesting.com
Printed in the USA
FSHW022156290921
85103FS